D0987184

SHE was extraordinary: a '[gen]ius" to British radical libe[ral] eighteenth century and a [...] petticoats" to most of her [contempo]raries. Mary Wollstonecraft (1759-97) was perhaps the first feminist, who began a lifelong crusade for female equality when she found herself needing to ask "Why was I not born a man, or why was I born at all?"

Maintaining that women do not have a history, except a passive and negative one, a "pre-history," Margaret George asserts that the life of Mary Wollstonecraft is an "important pre-historic document, perhaps in its offering of detail the most illuminating that we have."

Virginia Woolf remarked that Mary's life was an ". . . experiment from the start. . . . Every day she made theories by which life should be lived; and every day she came smack against the rock of other people's prejudices . . . the life of such a woman was bound to be tempestuous." Mrs. George's rich, interpretive recounting of Mary's life concentrates on "the woman held fast in," who felt herself to be, in spite of her many accomplishments, "a child to the end of the chapter." She points out that, despite her active rebellion, Mary could not completely escape the limited middle-class female situation.

MARGARET GEORGE is associate professor of history at the University of Illinois, Chicago Circle Campus.

ONE WOMAN'S
"SITUATION"

# ONE WOMAN'S "SITUATION"
### *A Study of Mary Wollstonecraft*
### by Margaret George

## UNIVERSITY OF ILLINOIS PRESS
*Urbana*      *Chicago*      *London*

# PREFACE

---

... women have a situation, not a history. ...

---

*O*NE of the most hard-minded statements that I have seen by a woman about women appeared recently in a *New Statesman* review (August 4, 1967) of a book entitled *The Petticoat Rebellion*. Perhaps the reviewer, Juliet Mitchell, was simply tired of works on women that culminated triumphantly in the Victorian "Movement"; or perhaps she meant it entirely when she wrote that the book was a "testimony to the impossibility of writing a descriptive history of women." Women, she went on, have a "situation," not a "continuous history. . . . In England they enter history at the point of suffrage agitation as a corporate group making its own self-limiting aims. Other than this, with a few individuals as exceptions, women's history has been that of their husband's or father's class. But faced with this absence of independent action do we not also have an absence of 'history'? There is no history of the passive and negative."

I admit a strong sympathy with those sentiments, a like weariness with accounts of the "Movement," a similar sense that the (tenacious, courageous) achievement of legal rights and the vote was a necessary but not at all sufficient lever to pry women out of their "situation." And I agree that the history of women as subjects of a continuing endeavor, of an active and conscious effort to create the conditions for their equality in a male-defined world is an impossibility, that we make do, instead, with a swift-told tale, the highest peaks of which are indeed "self-limiting aims."

Yet, putting my sympathy aside, Juliet Mitchell's blunt remarks are shortsighted. To begin, there can be, has been, history of the "passive and negative," which since the initial probings of J. S. Mill or August Bebel has accumulated to an impressive bulk in library card catalogs. From my point of view Simone de Beauvoir capped it with what is arguably the conceptually definitive examination of the female situation. Surely this is "history"—to trace the subjection and exploitation of women, or to outline the existential situation which has imprisoned them "in immanence." Surely it is even history in depth—to explore the ancient "otherness" that made women suspect, alien, and, especially, inferior to the dominant male; the division of labor which fixed women in domestic, i.e., servile, occupations; the economic dependence that has made parasites of the continuing majority of women; the social and political codes that assigned them places behind the scenes or in the galleries of the historical drama. Mlle de Beauvoir, moreover, flatly avowed her book—a *tour de force*, not least of hard, critical judgments—to be an analysis of passivity and abnegation, said it repeatedly, as in such passages as these:

Woman herself recognizes that the world is masculine on the whole; those who fashioned it, ruled it, and still dominate it today are men. As for her, she does not consider herself responsible for it; it is understood that she is inferior and dependent; she has not learned the lessons of violence, she has never stood forth as subject before the other members of the group. Shut up in her flesh, her home, she sees herself as passive before these gods with human faces who set goals and establish values. In this sense there is truth in the saying that makes her the "eternal child." . . . Not only is she ignorant of what constitutes a true action, capable of changing the face of the world, but she is lost in the midst of the world as if she were at the heart of an immense, vague nebula. . . . But, after all, to see things clearly is not her business, for she has been taught to accept masculine authority. So she gives up criticizing, investigating, judging for herself, and leaves all this to the superior caste. Therefore the masculine world seems to her a transcendent reality, an absolute. . . . A free individual blames only himself for his failures, he assumes responsibility for them; but everything happens to women through the agency of others, and therefore these others are responsible for her woes . . . she knows very well that she suffers as she does against her will: she is a woman without having been consulted in the matter. She dares not revolt; she submits unwillingly; her attitude is one of constant reproach. . . . She holds the entire world responsible because it has been made without her; she has been protesting against her condition since her adolescence, ever since her childhood. She has been promised compensations, she has been assured that if she would place her fortune in man's hands, it would be returned a hundredfold—and she feels she has been swindled. She puts the whole masculine universe under indictment. Resentment is the reverse side of dependence: when one gives all, one never receives enough in return.

Juliet Mitchell might rightly contend that she was denying the possibility of a "descriptive" history of women, not an existentialist treatise on their plight. But the logic of *The Second Sex* carries me along. At the end of 700-odd pages Beauvoir wrote that the "free woman is just being born." The whole of the book, its wealth of analysis and assertion, is then —and I think the author would consent to the term—but a *pre-history* of women. In the future, for Mlle de Beauvoir, lies the "authentically democratic society proclaimed by Marx [in which] there is no place for the Other." In the future lies the dawning of self-realization, the emergence of women as sovereign subjects of their lives, women who are economically free and equal as social producers, women grappling with life and making their mark upon it, assuming responsibility for the consequences of their, and others', actions. Says Beauvoir, "When we abolish the slavery of half of humanity, together with the whole system of hypocrisy that it implies, then the 'division' of humanity will reveal its genuine significance and the human couple will find its true form."

Thus—and why not follow the thought?—all the descriptions in card catalogs, like the whole of the analysis of *The Second Sex* that precedes the foreshadowing of the "reign of liberty in the midst of the world of the given," have been but pre-histories of women (not to say of men!). But in the future, if "by and through their natural differentiation men and women unequivocally affirm their brotherhood," that is, their humanity, if all become subjects of their lives and conscious directors of their reality, what will be the point of "female" history? The only history of women, in short, may be pre-history, precisely the history of the "passive and negative." And the only point in writing a history of women may be to penetrate the conditions of their enforced inferiority, and to chart the fits and starts and disappointments as well as the actual forward movement of their progress toward liberty.

And here, then, is a justification—in fact, an imperative—for histories of female passivity: there is both the necessity and the fascination of preserving the story of pre-historic women. Even the problem of method, of getting into a mostly source-less feminine world, fades away, at least in the "late" pre-historic age in Western societies since the eighteenth century. What Juliet Mitchell calls the "exceptions" to the submissive and inactive female mass are obvious and proper sources. Feminists, rebellious writers and artists, social deviants who refused the female role and struggled with their own sense of inferiority—such women (almost all of them: there are exceptions to the exceptions, Rosa Luxemburg, for one) were different from their silent and satisfied sisters in degree, not in kind, separated by their reactions to their situation, not by their situation in itself. Even the life of one such woman is an important pre-historic document, perhaps in its offering of detail the most illuminating that we have.

# CONTENTS

*M*

ONE WOMAN'S
"SITUATION"

*W*

# INTRODUCTION

## I

*E*VERY list of women who have made feminist history in the modern Western world includes if not begins with the name of Mary Wollstonecraft. Mary is an obvious pioneer; there were possible candidates before her—Aphra Behn, the talented playwright of the Restoration and the first English woman to support herself by her writing,[1] or Mary Astell, who, under the anonymity of "a Lover of her Sex," published in 1694 *A Serious Proposal to Ladies,* or a lady identifying herself only as "Sophia, a Person of Quality," whose pamphlet of 1739 was entitled *Woman not Inferior to Man*[2]—and she had ambitious contemporaries, including Catherine Macaulay, Olympe de Gouges, and Helen Maria Williams, but her position is unchallengeable. Christopher Hill, for example, writing about the mid–eighteenth century, uses her as his outer guide: "I am not sure that, in practice, women before Mary Wollstonecraft were conscious of the need for emancipation. Some may have resisted the pressures that degraded and humiliated them, but resistance was as yet hardly more than passive. . . ."[3]

Mary's essential life facts, *DNB*-style, are these—Wollstonecraft, Mary (1759–1797): contemporary and friend of Priestley, Price, and Paine; wife of William Godwin and mother of Mary Wollstonecraft Shelley (who, not her mother, was the

[1] See George Woodcock, *The Incomparable Aphra* (London, 1948), for an impressed, and lively, handling of that lady.

[2] A work often attributed to Lady Mary Wortley Montagu. See, for example, Florence Smith, *Mary Astell* (New York, 1916), p. 180. On the other hand, Doris Mary Stenton, *The English Woman in History* (London, 1957), p. 293, thinks the author was a male journalist.

[3] Christopher Hill, *Puritanism and Revolution: Studies in Interpretation of the English Revolution of the 17th Century* (London, 1958), p. 391.

3

creator of Frankenstein); author of *Rights of Woman*, feminist tract inspired by the soaring revolutionary enthusiasm of the 1790's; natural rights theorist, insisting on the equal humanity of men and women, demanding as a natural right women's equal access to education and opportunity. A less formal approach might begin with a touch of the melodramatic —Wollstonecraft, Mary (1759–1797): middle-class child fortunate only in that she grew up in almost a social vacuum; young woman whose life was a struggle—"warfare," she called it—for the independence of self-support, who decided with naive arrogance to be "an Author" to earn her living; maturing individual who declared proudly for the radicalism of the French Revolution and the freedom of her sex; woman-in-love who dropped everything she had won—to her near-destruction—for an obscure American named Gilbert Imlay, and who arrived just before her death at a compromise with love and independence with the apostle of Reason, the philosopher-anarchist, William Godwin.

But any sort of introduction would insist on the certainty of Mary's historical reputation, based on her stunning contribution to liberal ideology, indeed, to general modern consciousness. Christopher Hill's point, in the reference quoted above, occurs in an analytic discussion of Samuel Richardson's *Clarissa*, that eighteenth-century novel of bourgeois society, marriage, and moral attitudes. The plot is well enough known: Clarissa refuses to be sacrificed to the matrimonial market values of her rich and ambitious family, and as punishment is put in virtual solitary confinement. In her isolation she is tricked and seduced by the unscrupulous Lovelace, and thereby becomes, in Hill's words, "flawed goods" to a "commercial society." Deliberately she chooses to die, knowing that she has the "world's censure," but knowing too—and here is the core of her strength and stubborn will—the purity of her motives and behavior.[4] Clarissa is a passive rebel, forced by her private morality to fight her family, Lovelace, and society, and

[4] *Ibid.*, pp. 386, 385.

to do it with the weapon of their own (discarded) "religious orthodoxy." She lives and dies according to what Hill calls the "puritan conception of the infallible conscience." He quotes her words as her consciousness of the sources of her actions, of behavior that arose "principally from what offers to my own heart; respecting, as I may say, its own rectitude, its own judgement of the *fit* and the *unfit;* as I would, without study, answer *for* myself *to* myself, in the first place; to *him* [Lovelace] and to the *world,* in the *second* only. Principles that *are* in my mind; that I *found* there; implanted, no doubt, by the first gracious Planter: which therefore *impel* me, as I may say, to act up to them . . . let others act as they will by *me.*"[5] Mary Wollstonecraft is, of course, no real part of Hill's monographic purpose, his reference to her no more than an aside to an expository convenience, to the name of a new woman in bourgeois-capitalist society—as against the mutely miserable Clarissas of the mid–eighteenth century—whose historical activity as he sees it was allied with the "romantic individualist revolt."[6] The interesting thing, though, is the unlikeliness of Mary's accomplishment, given the fact that growing up in the 1760's and 1770's, she was much closer to Richardson's world than that of her daughter and Percy Bysshe Shelley. Forced, like Clarissa, by her own nature to oppose her will against her family, she built her individuality from the only materials at hand—from a religious orthodoxy, a promise of an ultimate heavenly reward for the virtuous, not so very different from Richardson's fictional account. But somehow Mary moved away from a passive rebellion and that "somehow" is the whole point of her story. Somehow her rebellion became an active, creative force that pushed her to live in critical opposition to her society. Somehow in the process of living, "in practice," she became conscious of her— and by extension, the feminine—"need for emancipation" and proceeded, through the choices of her adult life, to act out that emancipation. When, like Clarissa, Mary offered an explana-

[5] *Ibid.*, pp. 391–392.    [6] *Ibid.*, p. 391.

tion of her record, she had somehow achieved the striking contrast of calm assuredness, of an unself-conscious secularization of tone and intent:

> Those who are bold enough to advance before the age they live in, and to throw off, by the force of their own minds, the prejudices which the maturing reason of the world will in time disavow, must learn to brave censure. We ought not to be too anxious respecting the opinions of others. —I am not too fond of vindications. —Those who know me will suppose that I acted from principle. —Nay, as we in general give others credit for worth, in proportion as we possess it—I am easy with regard to the opinions of the *best* part of mankind. —I rest on my own.[7]

Mary's, then, was a full achievement. With the *Rights of Woman* she presented the issue of the historical and the continuing subjugation of women; at the very least with her book she made liberal ideologues aware of a major contradiction in their thought, in even their most radical blueprints for the progress of the human species. And because her feminism was the product of her life experience, she had to try to live it, not through an objectively rational plan but in the driving spontaneity of her decisions, choices, and actions. In both she was manifestly a first; her record thus is an important feminist document, a remarkable and open account of female response to the exhortation and promises of liberal individualism, of one woman's demand for equal opportunity for self-creation.

This is one level of entry into the story of Mary Wollstonecraft. Another is the observation that the most characteristic theme of her life was movement—sometimes straightforward, determined, and clear-sighted, sometimes blind, erratic, and confused. As an adolescent and young adult she knew well only what she didn't want, and that was the role that inevitably would make her both a victim of marital "tyranny" and a hostage to Mrs. Grundy; what she did want had to be discov-

---

[7] Mary Hays, "Mary Wollstonecraft," in *Annual Necrology, 1797–98* (London, 1800), p. 455.

ered in the trials of living. To be discovered, too, was what and who she was. Until she was in her mid-twenties her outward behavior would not have offended a Hannah More: escaping from an unfortunate family situation into the tight set of unpleasant alternatives that was the job market for a gentle-woman, Mary matter-of-factly accepted as the givens of a male-arranged society the little back-areas of gainful activity permitted the respectable working female. Maybe she resented such absolutes of her reality, but how could she think to change them, this daughter of Anglican orthodoxy and bour-geois familial convention?

After her thirtieth year Mary was the professional career woman, and with her *Rights of Woman*, the foremost feminist of her day, a "great genius" to radical liberals, a "hyena in petticoats" to anti-Jacobins.[8] Her published works of the 1790's provided a theoretical foundation for a century and a half of subsequent feminism. Her actions, her choices in that period, reflective of the singular confidence of the decade, put her far beyond the limits of respectability, made her incompre-hensibly shocking to her successors (the "unsex'd females") of the Victorian Movement. Mary's sisters during most of the nineteenth century would be the rare, aggressive rebels—Frances Wright, for example, or George Sand—who, like her, were considered "ripe for licentious indecorum," whose lives were judged indecent and deliberate defiance of "rules long established for the well government of society."[9] (Indeed, it was not till late in the century that even a feminist was willing to discuss Mary's sexual record of open extramarital relations and one child born out of wedlock.)[10]

[8] Quoted in William Godwin, *Memoirs of Mary Wollstonecraft*, W. Clark Durant, ed. (London and New York, 1927), Preface, p. xxxix; Mrs. Paget Toynbee, ed., *The Letters of Horace Walpole* (Oxford, 1905), XV, 337–338.

[9] *The European Magazine* (April, 1798), pp. 246, 251.

[10] See Elizabeth Robins Pennell, *The Life of Mary Wollstonecraft* (Boston, 1888). Godwin's biographer handled Mary ten years earlier as honestly as he could (and was the first to publish a number of her letters): see C. Kegan Paul, *William Godwin: His Friends and Contem-poraries* (London, 1876), 2 vols.

And the only possible category for Mary's two love affairs is an indistinct "modernity." When she met Gilbert Imlay she was thirty-four years old, an independent woman, she thought, freely entering into a free and equal relationship. What she discovered, in agony, was that she was not free and equal—and perhaps didn't even want to be. Mary came face to face with herself in the Imlay affair; some things she recognized, others she did not. But she learned a great deal in that near-devastating encounter—witness these words that she wrote sadly toward its end: "All the world is a stage, thought I; and few are there in it who do not play the part they have learnt by rote; and those who do not, seem marks set up to be pelted at by fortune; or rather as signposts, which point out the road to others, whilst forced to stand still themselves amidst the mud and dust."[11] It is important that Mary understood that she had been halted, after going so far and so fast, in the "mud and dust" of her own socially conditioned assumptions, impulses, and desires. Her relationship with William Godwin ended in marriage, and that was a kind of concession of defeat; but with Godwin she worked out an arrangement of semi-independence that might have been a kind of triumph.

The point is that in choosing an anomalous identity—independent woman in bourgeois society—Mary had chosen conditions for instability, uncertainty, and, often, pain. "I am not born to tread in the beaten track," she said, and surely that was true. Or was it? She could fight for and win economic independence; she could compete for professional status in London's male literary world; she could achieve celebration and fame. But perhaps what she wanted after all was to be her mother's daughter, to retreat with Gilbert Imlay to a domestic fireside and the raising of "six children." Or to bring Godwin (the architect of anarchism, the philosopher-father of the "authentic" man) to the altar, a love-object legally stamped "he is mine." Mary lived in two feminine worlds, the "passive and negative" and the rebelliously vocal; inevitably her life was, in

[11] Mary Wollstonecraft, *Letters Written during a Short Residence in Sweden, Norway, and Denmark* (London, 1796), p. 242.

Simone de Beauvoir's perfect phrase, an "inextricable confusion of revolt and complicity."[12]

## II

Not the least of Mary's possibilities as a biographical subject is the quality of her writings. She never wrote a line that was not revealing of herself, and she wrote many lines, some of them published before her death, some not; the bulk of the latter Godwin collected in his characteristically systematic way. In the months after she died it was Godwin's chief consolation to write the *Memoirs of the Author of "A Vindication of the Rights of Woman,"* the life account that was, he assured his readers, almost an autobiography, as though "from the mouth" of Mary herself. In four volumes of *Posthumous Works* he published her nonfiction and novels (of the latter, most importantly *The Wrongs of Woman; or, Maria,* which with her first work, *Mary, a Fiction,* supplies obvious actual details on her childhood and youth), and, equally valuable, the bulk of her letters to friends, to her publisher, and to Gilbert Imlay.[13] The only thing Godwin held back was the correspondence between Mary and himself; that appeared later, the crowning piece of a remarkably open record.

It is not that Mary's writing and thought were imperishable. Talent she most certainly had, and energy and a strong mind and strong opinions; she could write with power and a torrential force, especially when she was angry—in the *Rights of Men,* for instance, which was her reply to Burke's *Reflections on the French Revolution*—and some of the prose of her love

[12] Simone de Beauvoir, *The Second Sex,* H. M. Parshley, tr. (New York, 1953), p. 356.

[13] William Godwin, *Memoirs of the Author of "A Vindication of the Rights of Woman"* (London, 1798), p. 6. Godwin did not have Mary's letters to her sisters, Eliza and Everina, and early letters to friends. C. Kegan Paul published some of these and others have come to light since then. See Kenneth Neill Cameron, ed., *Shelley and His Circle, 1773–1822* (Cambridge, Mass., 1961), 2 vols., for the meticulous work that has gone into the collection and partial publication of Mary's letters.

letters, is poignantly lovely. As a writer of fiction, however, she worked with conscientious mediocrity within the worst conventions of her time; to the modern mind, her novels are the essence of sentimental nonsense, contrived plots of nobly suffering females and beastly males, all of them pretentiously and clumsily drawn. Her historical writing is the work of a self-educated amateur, concerned primarily (though justifiably, given the polemics of the 1790's) in spreading the ideology of liberal revolution. (Here Mary was completely outclassed by an original woman historian, Catherine Macaulay, whose *History of England from the Accession of James I to that of the Brunswick Line* is still judged a fine piece of work. As a matter of fact, some of the ideas of Mary's *Rights of Woman* were outlined in Macaulay's *Letters on Education*, which Mary reviewed and praised highly.) Nor was there anything exceptional in her instructional tracts or in her social criticism (other, of course, than their feminist thrust): convinced radical though she became, Mary remained wholly and unreflectively bourgeois, her middle-class assumptions apparently impervious to the explicit democracy of, for one, her acquaintance Thomas Paine.

But the point is that all of these works have a special quality, which is to say that Mary herself has a special quality. To the twentieth-century mind she is a true original and a true innocent, wonderfully deficient in self-consciousness about the often searing self-exposure of her words. Self-involved she was, excruciatingly so, to the extent that she could write herself without disguise into her fiction. Self-analytic and sometimes amazingly insightful, she explored herself in the most personal and private and yet ingenuous way. This is the appeal of the letters and novels and polemics: Mary unconsciously yet consciously exposed her life; all-innocent, she revealed herself and created herself on the printed page.

Since she became a fit subject for biography, Mary's writings have caught the attention of a variety of professionals. Elizabeth Robins Pennell's *Life*, from the 1880's, is chief among the first works, a solid, unflinchingly supportive narrative by a firm feminist. In 1927 Godwin's *Memoirs* got a fine new edition, by an editor who declared himself "the most faithful, constant, and unfailing lover Mary Wollstonecraft ever had";[14] in the 1930's Mary was the focus of a beautifully written, all too short essay by Virginia Woolf.[15] Subsequently she has been examined in an exhaustive scholarly work by Professor Ralph M. Wardle, fictionalized by the pseudonymous "George R. Preedy" as *This Shining Woman*, and psychoanalyzed by a hostile team of Freudian epigones.[16] (One feels the only possible sequel to the last two is a movie treatment with, say, Joan Crawford in the lead and playing with dramatic despair such scenes as Mary pacing in darkness and rain to soak her skirts before plunging into her thwarted death in the Thames.)

But I did not take a flippant attitude toward any of these books or their authors; all of them were testifying in some way to the broad interest and wide significance of the life of an extraordinary woman. Some of them I admired wholly—Virginia Woolf's essay, for one, a lovely thing, though only a tantalizing sketch. Mrs. Woolf recreated Mary in bold, brilliant strokes, portrayed her with sympathy and sensitivity, and ended with these words:

. . . Many millions have died and been forgotten in the hundred and thirty years that have passed since she was buried; and yet as we read her letters and listen to her arguments and consider her experiments, above all that most fruitful experiment, her relation with Godwin, and realise the high-handed and hot-blooded manner in which she cut her way to the quick of life, one form of immortality is hers undoubtedly: she is alive and active, she

[14] See Preface to *Memoirs*, p. xlv. It is this edition of Godwin's *Memoirs*, with its valuable Preface and Supplement in which the editor, W. Clark Durant, has gathered important information and documentation for Mary's story, that I will cite hereafter.

[15] Virginia Woolf, *The Second Common Reader* (London, 1932).

[16] Ralph M. Wardle, *Mary Wollstonecraft, a Critical Biography* (Lawrence, Kan., 1951); George R. Preedy, *This Shining Woman* (London, 1937); Ferdinand Lundberg and Marynia F. Farnham, *Modern Woman, the Lost Sex* (New York, 1947).

argues and experiments, we hear her voice and trace her influence even now among the living.[17]

And Professor Wardle's book—the most recent full biography of Mary—is readable, useful, and learned. Wardle painstakingly follows the course of Mary's activities, using every available lead to obscure, forgotten, or half-concealed sources in order to describe and appraise her and her writing. He is certainly on her side and "critical" only in the sense that he says at times she behaved arrogantly and egotistically, that she could be exasperating and wrong-headed. His biography is a kind of "Life and Times" (though the problem, it seems to me, is that Mary herself puts such demands on the biographer that he is hard put to squeeze in her contemporaries). His readers learn from every chapter of her story, gain general insights into the mid-century middle-class adolescent, the working spinster, the London (hired hand) journalist. After her literary triumphs, her activities and ideas are primary sources of English political radicalism: she was part of the international set of friends of the French Revolution who gathered in Paris, mostly around the Girondists, in the early 1790's. By 1794 her reactions reflect the disillusionment of her circle with the revolution as it moved from Jacobin "excesses" to Thermidorean opportunism (what Mary called the "aristocracy of riches"). Associated though she was with Godwin, she knew Blake, and was admired by Southey, Coleridge, and Hazlitt; indeed, in her most natural thoughts and inclinations she was a harbinger of English Romanticism. In developing these points, Wardle treats Mary as someone to whom he is attracted across the years, a fascinating individual and an interesting and informative historical personality—who just happens to be a woman.

Mary has gotten her share, then, of recent treatment from editors and biographers, most of them hard-working and talented in digging out and commenting on the facts of her life;

<hr />

[17] Woolf, *Second Common Reader,* p. 148 (Harvest edition, 1965, cited hereafter).

what she has not had is an interpreter. Turn-of-the-century feminists discovered her in her role as a founding member of their group, but that in itself limited their perspective. Virginia Woolf intuitively saw and understood a great deal more, though her essay was intended only as a descriptive vignette. Professor Wardle recorded *everything* about her, in a discursive method that seemed designed to avoid the essential woman.

I noted above that Mary had been psychoanalyzed in print, and in this, to be sure, is an interpretation: in their polemic on *Modern Woman, the Lost Sex,* Ferdinand Lundberg and Marynia Farnham chose Mary as a model of modern independent woman, the pioneer whose work was directly and immediately the "ideological" base of modern feminism (no historian of the nineteenth century would grant her that singular post). They briefly analyzed her childhood, diagnosed her as a compulsive neurotic, and concluded in one bound that all independent women have been sick, driven by their own insecurity and lack of confidence as women to deny their biological femininity, unconsciously forced to want to hurt themselves, their male oppressors, and established society. The Lundberg-Farnham version of Mary's life—her childhood "penis-envy" and hatred of "maleness" to which her *Rights of Woman* and all feminism "as an ideology" is "directly traceable," the love affairs in which she "threw herself" at men only to "strive for power" and "mastery" over them, the final episode in which she "drifted together" with William Godwin and died in childbirth (after, they noted, as if she had somehow deserved it, "eleven days of intense pain")[18]—produced a caricature, not only of Mary but also of Freudianism. These excerpts, for example, explained the relationship between Mary's "twisted personality" and the "psychopathology of feminism":

. . . Mary Wollstonecraft was an extreme neurotic of a compulsive type. . . . Out of her illness arose the ideology of femin-

[18] Lundberg and Farnham, *Modern Woman,* pp. 150–159 (Universal edition, 1959, cited hereafter).

ism, which was to express the feelings of so many women in years
to come.

Unconsciously . . . Mary and the feminists wanted to do injury
. . . to turn on men and injure them . . . however . . . men, in her
distorted view, could never be regarded as inferior to women.
Men were never, in her view, overcome by women. It was women
who were overcome by men. Underneath her aggressive writings,
Mary was a masochist like her mother, as indeed all the leading
feminist theorists were in fact. Aggressively Mary flung herself at
men. . . . The feminists were always doing this, thereby either
driving men away from them or capturing psychologically impaired males.

By behaving as she did Mary indicated, as we know from
clinical practice, that she was unconsciously seeking to deprive
the male of his power, to castrate him. Unconsciously she probably wished to emulate the heroine of Greek drama, Electra, and
kill her father, but this desire, although powerful, was powerfully
deflected as untenable. It came out only in her round scolding of
all men. The feminists have ever since symbolically slain their
fathers by verbally consigning all men to perdition as monsters.[19]

The authors of these words had, of course, some other
purpose (i.e., to provide psychoanalytic weapons in the post-
1945 campaign that returned the American woman to the
home) than a disinterested clinical study of the history of
Mary Wollstonecraft. And that is a pity. For the serious
interpreter, whether sympathetic or simply nonbiased, will
recognize the elements in Mary's story that fairly shout a
Freudian message. She did have a dreadful childhood, which she
talked about all her life, and bad relations with both parents.
Not even the Freudians know for sure whether or not she unconsciously wanted to kill either of them, though had she been
like Electra she might have wanted to kill her *mother*. (There
is a description of Mary, which Lundberg and Farnham probably missed, by a European woman, Madeleine Schweitzer,
who knew her in Paris. Mrs. Schweitzer wrote in her journal
that Mary "was so intolerant that she repulsed those women

[19] *Ibid.*, pp. 159–161.

who were not inclined to be subservient to her," though "to her servants, her inferiors, and the wretched in general, she was gentle as an angel.")[20] It is obvious that Mary had deep difficulties in competition with women, and that men, love, and sex were problems all her life; and with Imlay, at least, she had what could only be called a neurotic episode. All her life, too, she fretted over baffling emotional reactions; a recurring cry of anxiety was her "I know not myself."

Mary's interpreter would be forced, then, to come to grips with the facts of her neurotic behavior (and would half-expect to find similar evidence in the lives of subsequent feminists), but surely it can be done in more useful ways than the Lundberg-Farnham effort. Actually, one could stay within a Freudian conceptual apparatus and propose that Mary's "neurosis" —out of her conflict with bad parental models—was a creative force, the stimulus for a sublimating search for a finer structure of human relations. Virginia Woolf would have boggled at a picture of a Mary motivated by unconscious drives both aggressive and masochistic, and predetermined to seek in fixated futility for resolution of a childhood trauma, but she was nevertheless on a Freudian track in her account. Mary's life, wrote Mrs. Woolf, was "an experiment from the start. . . . Every day she made theories by which life should be lived; and every day she came smack against the rock of other people's prejudices. Every day too—for she was no pedant, no coldblooded theorist—something was born in her that thrust aside her theories and forced her to model them afresh." It was the "conflict" of the "contradictions" in her that motivated Mary, and in truth the "life of such a woman was bound to be tempestuous."[21]

But I would leave the Freudians altogether—with their ahistorical analytic structures, their attempts to define a life by uniquely determining infantile experience—to explore and explain the working out of Mary's neurotic tensions. It seems so

[20] Godwin, *Memoirs*, Supplement, p. 247.
[21] Woolf, *Second Common Reader*, p. 144.

obvious: only the larger and qualitatively different interpretation does descriptive and analytic justice to her life.

In Mary's world the *embourgeoisement* of a century had
dramatically narrowed the roles and choices of women qual-
ifying for gentility (capitalism, that "shaping destiny of economic forces working through conventions of society on
human character. . .").[22] Women, of course, had no political
rights, no areas of public responsibility for the talented even of
the patriciate (not that most cared, perhaps: Lady Mary Wortley Montagu deplored women's lack of education but she was
"satisfied" with their "state of subjection" in public life, content to leave the burdens of "authority" to men).[23] With
capitalist organization, which made the (male) individual the
basic unit of society, economic opportunities still open in the
seventeenth century to women within a family setting were
closing inexorably: few women now were helpmates and thus
respected equals in trades and businesses with their husbands.
In place of participation and partnership, "the wife of the
prosperous capitalist tended to become idle, the wife of the
skilled journeyman lost her economic independence and became his unpaid domestic servant. . . ."[24] The prospects of
unmarried women were almost as limited: as Mary herself
observed, the several trades "left to women" were "gradually
falling into the hands of the men"—in the clothing industry,
for example, or midwifery, that traditionally female occupation. For the gentlewoman, single and unsupported, there was
what Jane Austen would describe as the "penance and mortifi-

[22] Robert Palfrey Utter and Gwendolyn Bridges Needham, *Pamela's
Daughters* (New York, 1936), p. 41.
[23] Mary Wortley Montagu, *The Works of the Right Honorable Lady
Mary Wortley Montagu, Including her Correspondence, Poems and
Essays* (5 vols., London, 1803), IV, 161.
[24] Alice Clark, *Working Life of Women in the Seventeenth Century*
(London, 1919), pp. 307, 196-197, 235. See Utter and Needham, *Pamela's
Daughters*, pp. 20-24, and *passim*; Ian Watt, *The Rise of the Novel*
(Berkeley and Los Angeles, 1964), pp. 142-146; Daniel Defoe, *The
Complete English Tradesman* and *Essay upon Projects* (London, 1726,
1697), is a basic source for all of the above.

cation"[25] of being a governess or a companion to the wealthy; so few middle-class girls dared to think of professional status that Mary, the ambitious journalist, "trembled" at being a "new genus" in living by her pen. Denied the specialized training and skills essential to a productive role, shut out from formal education, consigned to idleness and "charming dependence" (in the middle and upper classes; in the lower she was "beaten down into sweated trades"),[26] woman was redefined in this emerging modern world as an explicitly inferior "other." "No where," wrote Lady Mary Montagu, "is the sex treated with such contempt as in England."[27]

In manners and conduct the young woman of Mary's world was to become something fitting to her essential irrelevance, something close to an image drawn by Dr. John Gregory in his instructional essay entitled *A Father's Legacy to his Daughters* (a book popular and influential enough that Mary used it as a chief target in her *Rights of Woman*). The girl Dr. Gregory hoped his daughters would be was a simple organism: she would demonstrate a convincing piety, a noncritical, nonquestioning religious faith that was both good in itself and necessary to assure men of "one of their principal securities for that female virtue in which they are most interested." In her behavior she would show a "modest reserve" and a "retiring delicacy"; she would be mostly "silent in company"—for "wit" was a "most dangerous talent"—and if she happened to "have any learning" she would "keep it a profound secret, especially from the men."[28] The perfection of these qualities led obviously to the one decisive question of her life—to marry or not. She would not indulge in romantic notions of love: "What is commonly called love, among you," Dr. Gregory explained to his daughters, "is rather gratitude, and a partiality to the man who prefers you to the rest of your sex: and such a man you often marry, with little of either personal esteem or

[25] Jane Austen, *Emma* (London, 1816), p. 131 (Signet edition, 1964).
[26] Clark, *Working Women*, p. 302.    [27] Montagu, *Works*, IV, 161.
[28] John Gregory, *A Father's Legacy to his Daughters* (London, 1816), pp. 17–24.

affection." Indeed, he said, "a woman in this country has very little probability of marrying for love." Ideally, the young woman had some element of choice, as in fact Dr. Gregory's daughters did: he assured them if they did not marry they would not be left in the "forlorn and unprotected situation of an old maid," would not lose the "ease and independence" they had in his home; thus they had no reason to marry hastily, to a "fool" or a "tyrant." But inevitably, and Dr. Gregory clinched the point by the preponderant weight of his advice on the subject, the young woman would choose to be chosen for marriage.[29]

Marriage, then, was literally the only female destiny—as one commentator puts it, no other way "was honorable, was approved, was even tolerable."[30] Outside of it was the absolute desperation of prostitution (unthinkable for any but a Moll Flanders) and the almost equally desperate situation of the "old maid," which by Mary's day (and not long after Defoe's) was the definition of uselessness. Women in marriage were possessions in a market society; women outside of marriage were ciphers, victims of their economic helplessness, or burdens to their relatives and themselves.

This was the female condition that Mary Wollstonecraft, unhappy, "neurotic" girl-child, rebelled against. In the circuitous course of her rebellion she came to, stumbled into, the articulation of *The Rights of Woman*. She may not have understood much of social and economic forces or much about the bourgeois structure of exploitation, but in her book she described her world and her conscious perception of its inadequacy, and demanded, in impeccable liberal language, that it be changed.

She wanted women to emancipate themselves from the "galling yoke of sovereign man" that had been their burden since the separation of Adam's rib. She wanted them to realize the degradation of the male-imposed feminine image, the "car-

[29] *Ibid.*, pp. 61, 80, and *passim*.
[30] See Utter and Needham, *Pamela's Daughters*, pp. 20–24.

dinal virtues" of which were "gentleness, docility, and a spaniel-like affection," plus a sexual accessibility that made them the "toy of man." She wanted women to create themselves and their individual existences, as men did, by their "*own* exertions," to know that satisfaction came in the mastering of hard intellectual and practical tasks. She wanted them to "struggle with the world" rather than to retreat in appealing helplessness and ignorance to their "trivial occupations and pursuits." Above all, she wanted them to escape the trap of "sensuality" that it amused men to concede was the source of female "power" over them, to reach the ultimate "virtue" that was power "over themselves."[31]

This was Mary's vision—and it was a revolutionary vision, the implications of which cut into the core-value of bourgeois society, carried a critical insight into a society in which people related to one another as objects, in which each attempted to use the other as an instrument of his will. It was also a set of imperatives for her own action, a way of life she tried to live, though with uneven success: power over herself, especially, Mary only uncertainly had. Which was neurotic—the vision, or the confused activity?

Mary's childhood emotional problems, her resentments and frustrations, her consequent maladjustment, were without question one condition for her adult feminism. But those emotional problems were also the most direct cause of her erratic adult commitment, of her inability to live her vision steadily and purposefully. They clouded her insights, deflected her projects, upset her decisions, shook her determinations; they kept her (albeit kicking and squirming) a prisoner of conventional codes and roles and values. They kept her a bourgeois woman and, as she saw it in a flash of melancholy self-analysis, a "child to the end of the chapter."

[31] Mary Wollstonecraft, *A Vindication of the Rights of Woman* (London, 1792), pp. 68, 65, 66, 108, 134; *Thoughts on the Education of Daughters; with Reflections on Female Conduct, in the more important Duties of Life* (London, 1787), pp. 100, 101.

Like Lundberg and Farnham, but with very different purpose, I, too, propose Mary Wollstonecraft as an excellent model of "modern woman." Admittedly she was a special woman even in Dr. Gregory's terms: she was never modestly reserved and retiring; she talked excessively in company; and when she acquired some learning she delighted in parading it, especially before the men. Her talents, her ambitions, her accomplishments—these things have long entered Mary in the traditional historical record; but even these have a different perspective within a close concentration on the woman held fast in, and indeed defining, the woman's "situation."

*Chapter One*

# THE CHILD

. . . Neglected in every respect, and left to the operations of her own mind, she considered every thing
that came under her inspection, and learned to think.
*Mary, a Fiction*

One is not born, but rather becomes, a woman.
*The Second Sex*

MARY WOLLSTONECRAFT was in her mid-thirties when
she told William Godwin the story of her past and
thus provided him with the primary sources that
he would use after her death in the *Memoirs,* which in turn
would be taken as basic data by all of Mary's subsequent
biographers. In her telling, in looking back to her childhood,
Mary was concerned with evoking moods, illustrating patterns,
making a case; that is to say, she was not interested in precision
in her vital statistics or in what she doubtless considered the
minutia of exact description. She wasn't sure, for example,
whether she was born in London or in the "old mansion" on a
farm in the Epping Forest that she remembered from about the
age of five. She wasn't sure of—and apparently didn't care
about—the occupational activity of her father in the year of
1759. It was enough to begin that she was the second child and
first daughter of Edward John and Elizabeth Wollstonecraft, a
young couple who had at some point inherited the impressive
sum of 10,000 pounds from her paternal grandfather, a "rich
Spitalfields manufacturer," and who, about the time she was
born, had gone into farming, "rather perhaps as an amusement
than a business."[1]

[1] Godwin, *Memoirs,* p. 8.

Modern scholarship has both tidied up and corrected these points: Mary was born in London in April of 1759, when her father, a master-weaver like his father, was listed in city directories as living at "*Primrose-street Bishopsgate* without." The records show that she was baptized in May at her parents' parish church, St. Botolph, Bishopsgate, as the next Wollstonecraft baby, Elizabeth, would be in 1763.[2] That evidence suggests that Mary was about four when Edward John, bold with the inheritance from his successful and thrifty weaver-sire, attempted the economic and social leap (much less amusing than audacious) into the status of gentleman-farmer.

Further, Mary's testimony does not directly state the slow strangulation of that probably quite serious ambition. Edward John was no master of agriculture: the fine patrimony trickled away in a succession of unprofitable farming ventures—three of them, requiring three moves, came in the first five years after 1763. In his frustration Edward John took to drink and bullying his wife and an eventual brood of six children; disappointed in whatever expectations she might have had, Elizabeth became the beaten wife, hopelessly, spinelessly waiting out her days. Indeed, as a functioning unit the family was beaten: by Mary's twenty-first year Edward John was a drunken, self-admitted failure, and Elizabeth had died as passively and unremarkably as she had lived. Only the eldest son, Edward, had been prepared for a profession (in the law); the other children, desperate to get out, had no hope of assistance —two younger sons with uncertain portions and no career plans, three girls with dowries (had they been arranged) entangled with parental debts.

For the biographer this is necessary information, necessary as a silently oppressive backdrop to the special kind of evidence Mary gave about her childhood to Godwin and in her novels, *Mary, a Fiction* and *The Wrongs of Woman; or, Maria.* It was apparently not so to Mary: her story was an intensely personal, in fact totally egocentric, tale of painful

---

[2] Cameron, ed., *Shelley and His Circle*, I, 39–41.

psychological pressures. If the Wollstonecrafts had pleasant moments and pleasant memories, if, in the early days before Edward John lost hope in gentlemanly farming, there were good times in comfortable farmhouse sufficiency and tussling country fun, Mary had forgotten them all. Or, on another tack, if her brothers and sisters were equally damaged by their parental environment, she was not interested in that. Nor would she be distracted into recollection of external matters: she did not mention childhood friends or family visitors and acquaintances; she had no direct information about her parents' social values, political views, or religious attitudes; she made no reference to crucial practical concerns—the conditions of her father's land purchases and his operation of the farms, her mother's management of the household. (The last omissions are significant: Mary's indifference to practical affairs suggests some measure of the unconsciously accepted economic security of the family; the father had not made them rich but neither did he threaten them with destitution. Only in such social and financial certainty could Mary have afforded the luxury of concentration on herself. Money and debt would be a problem in her future but never an anxiety.) What Mary remembered, what she related to Godwin, what she described in her novels, with single-minded repetition, was her own suffering. Her early life, she insisted again and again, was a constant battle, a constant conflict with her family, a constant conflict with her own ambivalent feelings about her family, a constant round of punishing relationships.

The narrative of the *Memoirs*—in Godwin's prose, but on his vow faithfully reproducing Mary's own words—plunges immediately into this self-preoccupation, and into the perceived sources of the child-Mary's unhappiness. The passage following is important in its totality; within it are the themes of Mary's self-analysis, those things she considered essential to an explanation and understanding of her adult personality:

I am doubtful whether the father of Mary was bred to any profession [though we know that he was a weaver]; but, about the time of her birth, he resorted . . . to the occupation of farming. He was of a very active, and somewhat versatile disposition, and so frequently changed his abode, as to throw some ambiguity upon the place of her birth. She told me, that the doubt in her mind in that respect, lay between London, and a farm upon Epping Forest, which was the principal scene of the first five years of her life. Mary was distinguished in early youth, by some portion of that exquisite sensibility, soundness of under-standing, and decision of character, which were the leading features of her mind through the whole course of her life. She experienced in the first period of her existence, but few of those indulgences and marks of affection, which are principally calcu-lated to sooth the subjection and sorrows of our early years. She was not the favourite of either her father or mother. Her father was a man of a quick, and impetuous disposition, subject to alternate fits of kindness and cruelty. In his family he was a despot, and his wife appears to have been the first, and most submissive of his subjects. The mother's partiality was fixed upon the eldest son [Edward], and her system of government relative to Mary, was characterized by considerable rigour. She, at length, became convinced of her mistake, and adopted a different plan with her younger daughters. When in the Wrongs of Woman, Mary speaks of "the petty cares which obscured the morning of her heroine's life; continual restraint in the most trivial matters; unconditional submission to orders, which, as a mere child, she soon discovered to be unreasonable, because inconsistent and contradictory; and the being often obliged to sit, in the presence of her parents, for three or four hours together, without daring to utter a word"; she is, I believe, to be considered as copying the outline of the first period of her own existence.

But it was in vain that the blighting winds of unkindness or indifference, seemed destined to counteract the superiority of Mary's mind. It surmounted every obstacle; and by degrees, from a person little considered in the family, she became in some sort its director and umpire. The despotism of her education cost her many a heart-ache. She was not formed to be the contented and unresisting subject of a despot; but I have heard her remark more than once, that, when she felt she had done wrong, the reproof or chastisement of her mother, instead of being a terror to her, she found to be the only thing capable of reconciling her to herself.

The blows of her father, on the contrary, which were the mere ebullitions of a passionate temper, instead of humbling her roused her indignation. Upon such occasions she felt her superiority and was apt to betray marks of contempt. The quickness of her father's temper, led him sometimes to threaten similar violence towards his wife. When that was the case, Mary would often throw herself between the despot and his victim, with the purpose to receive upon her own person the blows that might be directed against her mother. She has even laid whole nights upon the landing-place near their chamber-door, when, mistakenly, or with reason, she apprehended that her father might break out into paroxysms of violence. The conduct he held towards the members of his family, was of the same kind as that he observed towards animals. He was for the most part extravagantly fond of them; but, when he was displeased, and this frequently happened, and for very trivial reasons, his anger was alarming. Mary was what Dr. Johnson would have called, "a very good hater." In some instance of passion exercised by her father to one of his dogs, she was accustomed to speak of her emotions of abhorrence, as having risen to agony. . . .[3]

Mary's novels, *Mary, a Fiction* and *The Wrongs of Woman; or, Maria,* use as plot background the whole of the structure and many of the details of the Godwin narrative. Both are irresistibly suggestive sources for a biographer, even though there are clear problems involved: in *Mary,* for example, the heroine is from a wealthy family and socially superior by far to the Wollstonecrafts; the mother is probably consciously modelled on Lady Kingsborough, by whom Mary was employed as governess when she wrote the book. But Mary's memories and perceptions of, her emotional troubles within, her own family dominate both books. This from *Maria* describes the brute-tyrant of a father, the submissively suffering mother: "His orders were not to be disputed; and the whole house was expected to fly at the word of command. He was to be instantaneously obeyed, especially by my mother, whom he very benevolently married for love; but took care to remind

[3] Godwin, *Memoirs*, pp. 8-12.

her of the obligation when she dared, in the slightest instance, to question his absolute authority."[4] Or, in the following from *Mary*, with the mother made an invalid (as Mary's mother was in the last year of her life), there is allusion to scenes that Godwin mentioned, of Mary lying "whole nights" outside her parents' door to try to save her mother from her father's violence: "[Her father] treated [her mother] with indifference; but when her illness at all interfered with his pleasures, he expostulated in the most cruel manner, and visibly harassed the invalid. Mary would then assiduously try to turn his attention to something else; and when sent out of the room would watch at the door, until the storm was over, for unless it was, she could not rest."[5] An elder brother, who could only be based on Mary's own Edward, gets elaborate treatment in *Maria:*

My eldest brother, it is true, as he grew up, was treated with more respect by my father; and became in due form the deputy-tyrant of the house. The representative of my father, a being privileged by nature, a boy, and the darling of my mother, he did not fail to act like an heir apparent. Such indeed was my mother's extravagant partiality, that, in comparison with her affection for him, she might be said not to love the rest of her children. Yet none of the children seemed to have so little affection for her. Extreme indulgence had rendered him so selfish, that he only thought of himself; and from tormenting insects and animals, he became the despot of his brothers, and still more of his sisters.[6]

Mary was reluctant to let this absorbing theme go: "My brother Robert . . . might truly be termed the idol of his parents, and the torment of the rest of the family. Such indeed is the force of prejudice, that what was called spirit and wit in him, was cruelly repressed as forwardness in me."[7] Like the

---

[4] William Godwin, *Posthumous Works of the Author of "A Vindication of the Rights of Woman," The Wrongs of Woman; or, Maria, a Fragment* (4 vols., London, 1799), I, 142.

[5] Mary Wollstonecraft, *Mary, a Fiction* (London, 1788), pp. 15–16.

[6] Godwin, *Posthumous Works, Maria,* I, 143.

[7] *Ibid.,* p. 145.

real Edward, the fictional Robert was articled to an attorney, though he came home every weekend "to astonish my mother by exhibiting his attainments." Even then, he "seemed to take a peculiar pleasure in tormenting and humbling me; and if I ever ventured to complain of this treatment to either my father or mother, I was rudely rebuffed for presuming to judge of the conduct of my eldest brother."[8]

Again, in the record of Mary's childhood there is no break in this preoccupation with the Wollstonecraft domestic drama, involving always and only (in her novels Mary does not use her younger siblings as fictional subjects) father and mother, brother and self. The single, perpetual subject of the drama is, of course, the unhappy girl at center stage whose qualities the sympathetic reader is invited to contemplate. She is a powerful personality, a child to be reckoned with: an active, aggressive child who preferred the "hardy sports of her brothers" to the "dolls and the other toys usually appropriated to the amusement of female children";[9] a superior child, bright, intelligent, sensitive to nuances of thought and emotion; a child volatile like her father, quick to express emotions; a child who was the victim of anger and physical punishment which came so early and so often that she learned not to fear it; a child who identified with other targets of irrational brutality, with beggars "driven from the gate without being relieved,"[10] with her father's dogs, with perhaps above all her mother; yet a child of strong will who refused to be browbeaten and who had contempt for those who allowed themselves to be cowed; a child thwarted in her need for affection and approval, whose perhaps strongest feeling was a sense of the injustice of her mother's preference for her elder brother.

The father, the mother, the brother are the antagonists of the scene, objects through the subject's consciousness (with Mary directing, therefore, even a speculative development of their qualities). Elizabeth Wollstonecraft was the steady par-

[8] *Ibid.*, p. 152.  [9] Godwin, *Memoirs*, p. 13.
[10] Wollstonecraft, *Mary*, p. 16.

ent, the chief disciplinarian whose "system of government" of her eldest daughter was "characterized by considerable rigour," who imposed "continual restraint in the most trivial matters" and demanded "unconditional submission to orders." Mary felt her not only harsh but cold and unapproachable: "She had once, or twice, told her little secrets to her mother; they were laughed at, and she determined never to do it again. In this manner was she left to reflect on her own feelings."[11] It was her mother's love that Mary most desperately wanted, and her mother's unloving treatment that most cruelly hurt her: her favoritism for Edward gave Mary "exquisite pain, —and produced a kind of habitual melancholy, led her into a fondness for reading tales of woe. . . ."[12] So it is understandable that Elizabeth was a strong enough figure to influence Mary: "When she felt she had done wrong, the reproof or chastisement of her mother, instead of being a terror to her, she found to be the only thing capable of reconciling her to herself." And yet Elizabeth was also a dependent and a subordinate, a childlike person whom the father abused, so that Mary, in a reversal of roles, wanted frantically to protect her.

Nowhere in the *Memoirs* or the novels is there a suggestion that Mary had a feminine model other than her mother during her childhood and most of her adolescence. It was a long, decisive period that Elizabeth had to try to recreate her own image in her eldest daughter. One wishes Mary had worked more with dialogue in her autobiographical novels. She might thereby have given a clear reproduction of Elizabeth counseling her daughter to submission to and acceptance of the hard lot that was God's will for the female. Godwin's account of the mother's "system of government" indicates a conventional attempt on the one hand to curb a strong-willed child, on the other to train the hopefully marriage-bound girl to silence and obedience. Was Mary's childish impulsiveness judged as sinful behavior, was she a Maggie Tulliver, belittled in her tom-boyishness, ridiculed as an improper girl, undermined in her femi-

[11] *Ibid.*, pp. 16–17.    [12] *Ibid.*, p. 14.

ninity? What is sure is that Mary's feelings toward her mother were a study in contradiction: dominated on one side by an infantile, insatiable need for love, and a desperate desire, which would be clear in late adolescence, to do and be the things that would earn that love; on the other, by resentment, rebellious-ness, and rejection of the mother's identity of passivity and resignation.

Edward is a stereotype, the big brother bully who pulls off flys' wings and torments cats and girls, but his chief character-istic is that he is—male. There is no need for the concept of penis-envy, which even the neo-Freudians have relegated to a secondary effect: the traumatic reaction of the little girl at the sight of the male genitals occurs, says Dr. Helene Deutsch, only when "a long chain of earlier experiences" have predis-posed the child to a sense of her inferiority, in which case the discovery of her anatomical inadequacy is a "rationalization of it, so to speak."[13] Mary gave a steady concurrence on the point: from her earliest awareness she *knew* she was slighted for Edward, knew he was their parents' center of love and approval; her recognition of his maleness, whenever it oc-curred, merely explained this clear injustice. Of course, then, she envied and resented the parent-sanctioned superiority of her brother (as she would later envy and resent the just as real socially sanctioned superiority of the male sex). And if her parents, especially her mother, admonished her or tried to make her feel guilty for her envy, she remained unrepentantly bitter, certain that she was the undeserving victim of a vi-ciously irrational partiality.

In Godwin's narrative Mary's father gets a disproportionate amount of descriptive attention—this mercurial master who loved "extravagantly," was "active" and "versatile," "quick and impetuous," of a "passionate temper," prone to "alternate fits of kindness and cruelty." Mary, and Godwin too, undoubt-edly saw the father as the key to her adult self, her feminism

[13] Helene Deutsch, *Psychology of Women: A Psychoanalytic Inter-pretation* (2 vols., New York, 1944), I, 319–320.

and hatred of the male tyrant. Certainly by the time she wrote
*Mary* (in her late twenties), she was convinced that she detested this "systematic tyrant" with his uncontrollable drunken
rages, his unthinking, casual brutality, who was, moreover, as
she realized from her teens, a weakling and a failure in society's
terms. But for a good many important years Edward John
Wollstonecraft was the center and focus of Mary's world, the
god for whose attention she competed, probably strenuously
and passionately. He was her male model, and her image of
power and freedom—of the freedom, that is, to exercise one's
will without restraint. If she hated the way he used his power
and freedom, the way he treated her mother especially, she
hated just as much the supine life-attitude of the powerless.
She saw herself in her father, saw warmth and passion and
spontaneity as her deepest nature, her "former nature," as she
much later told Gilbert Imlay, which had been "suppressed" in
her youth, presumably by her mother.[14] Somehow Mary
learned to live and to love, passionately and generously (in
contrast to her mother's niggardly, cautious allocation of herself), and one suspects it was from this father whose affection
was bestowed as unreservedly as his anger.

With her father, then, as with her mother, Mary had a hard
dilemma, though as an adolescent she apparently worked out a
partial answer. She wrote in *Mary* (an amazing passage,
suggestive of the values of Elizabeth Wollstonecraft) that her
heroine was "violent in her temper; but she saw her father's
faults and would weep when obliged to compare his temper
with her own. —she did more; artless prayers rose to Heaven
for pardon, when she was conscious of having erred; and her
contrition was so exceedingly painful, that she watched diligently the first movements of anger and impatience to save
herself of this cruel remorse."[15] If she had not swallowed her

---

[14] Roger Ingpen, ed., *The Love Letters of Mary Wollstonecraft to
Gilbert Imlay* (London, 1908), XXXII. There are two other editions of
the letters to Imlay: Godwin's edition in the *Posthumous Works* (1799),
and that of C. Kegan Paul (London, 1879).

[15] Wollstonecraft, *Mary*, p. 12.

mother's line of submission and quietude—with the promise of
a heavenly reward, God's kingdom for the meek—Mary had
convinced herself, with Elizabeth's help, that such a father as
Edward John was an unworthy love object. Or she had half-
convinced herself: "Perhaps," she wrote in her first published
piece, "a delicate mind is not susceptible of a greater misery,
putting guilt out of the question, than what must arise from
the consciousness of loving a person [of] whom their reason
does not approve."[16]

It is an unpleasant, ugly drama Mary built out of her childhood: the father, lord of the manor, using his property—wife,
children, dogs—according to his momentary mood and whim;
the mother humble before him, yet capricious with her dependents, alternately seeking compensatory love in petting and
indulging her eldest son and venting her resentments on her
eldest daughter. Isolation and self-centeredness, each one en-
capsulated, shut off from the others and incapable of sustained
loving or empathetic relationships—Mary's picture of the
Wollstonecraft family is almost an overillustration of the de-
humanized characteristics of Professor C. B. MacPherson's
"possessive market society."[17] Mary took from that family
insights appropriate to the macrocosm of her society: every-
one was on his/her own in the atomized arena of human
action; the strong were likely to use their power irresponsibly,
selfishly, and hurtfully; weakness and dependence meant bondage, humiliation, and pain; and love, approval, and acceptance
were nobody's rightful portion (unless one happened to be a
particularly favored male). The last point contained for Mary
a further lesson: there were no rewards for femaleness—she
saw none in the example of her mother, nor did she feel she
had received any from her father. Prestige, and love, were for
male doers and achievers. She would then be boylike, except
that over her was her mother, threatening further withdrawal

---

[16] Wollstonecraft, *Thoughts on the Education of Daughters*, pp. 82–83.
[17] C. B. MacPherson, *The Political Theory of Possessive Individualism*
(Oxford, 1962).

of love from the ungirlish girl and holding up a vague promise of some future, undefined prize for the truly feminine.

Perhaps it is stressing the obvious to point out that Mary's problems were terribly uncomplicated, that they were "female" problems. As a girl, without the natural encouragement a boy would have to substitute, to sublimate, to relate effectively to a larger world, she was obliged to chew on her family situation, to nurse her grievances, to probe her wounds. Love and the absence of love, envy and resentment and bitterness about the privileges of the chosen ones, impotence to do anything about her unprivileged status—these things were Mary's towering realities. She should have been (and sometimes was) a most unpleasant woman, suspicious and distrustful, self-pitying and passive, sure that adversity was her undeserving lot, sure that things were done to her in a cold, unjust world—in fact, a new Elizabeth Wollstonecraft, or a pinched, complaining spinster as her sisters would be.

Or, to follow the same line of thought on another, perhaps again obvious, level, Mary's lifetime obsession with the parent-brother complex of her early years was in itself the most painfully negative effect: she was so involved in the felt injustice and rejection of her childhood that she was limited in the development of mind and emotions, indeed, crippled in imagination. One proof of the narrowness of her perspectives is that *Maria*, that bad piece of semifiction that she worked on just before her death, was once again a re-hash of her childhood and youth, its chief distinction from the earlier *Mary* that it had more subplots, since by then Mary was more aware of the social wrongs done to women of the lower as well as the middle class. She was a creative writer only when her very personal material fit creatively into the time and historical scene, as in the reply to Burke or *The Rights of Woman*, or when she could forget herself in sensitive description of her natural surroundings, as in the *Letters from Sweden*. From this point of view, the one thing to be said for Mary's fixation on childish hostilities and resentments, determining as it did the areas of her adult interests and preoccupations and accomplishments, is that it was also obviously the motive power behind her adult drive and ambition. One can concentrate a great deal of energy on a problem so narrowly delineated, on an enemy —men—so clearly identified, on a goal—independence (which for Mary meant the state of not being dependent on a man)— so necessary.

And yet there is this contradiction in her childhood: if it constricted her choices, at the very same time it enlarged them. The furious child who stood up to her father, who was more incensed by than resigned to the reality of male superiority, who refused the identities of both father and mother as incompatible with her own drives, was too active to be properly receptive. She was so obsessed with her sense of deprivation, so busy reacting, judging, and rejecting that she had neither time nor energy for the important social lessons she should have been learning as a middle-class daughter. There were basic attitudes she could not fail to absorb from her family and from the varieties of community life that the Wollstonecrafts had; by her teen-age years she knew something of the rules for female behavior, something of the limits of her possibilities, something of the level of expectations ahead of her. But still, out of the experience of her childhood, both Mary and her future emerged peculiarly unformed, unshaped, undirected.

And out of that experience, then, she prepared to be a self-creator, to find her own form, shape, and direction. She was prepared, too, to be entirely egocentric—not that that, surely, made her unique: in Mary's lifetime the trickle of testimony in and about the first-person singular would be growing to a flood of confessional self-examination. A message about that social phenomenon of bourgeois individualism is in the opening chapter of Mary's story, in the development of a strong-willed little girl in an environment which gave her nothing to think about but herself.

*Chapter Two*

# THE ADOLESCENT

---

> . . . I am a little singular in my thoughts of love and
> friendship; I must have the first place or none.
>
> Letter to Jane Arden

> At ten or twelve years of age most little girls are truly
> "*garçons manqués*"—that is to say, children who lack
> something of being boys . . . they feel it as a depriva-
> tion and an injustice . . . they give themselves up to
> gloomy and romantic daydreams . . . they are jealous,
> sensitive, demanding.
>
> *The Second Sex*

---

### I

*I*N her early teens Mary was a solitary, introspective
girl, prone to melancholy, and proud in her loneliness and expectation of rejection, yet child enough
and aggressive enough to vent her resentment at her unfulfilled
needs for love and proper valuation. Granted, this may not be
the whole story: writing to an old friend five or six years later,
she remembered the "merry days" when they laughed "from
noon 'till night," when they "eagerly told every girlish secret
of [their] hearts," "peaceful days" when she, Mary, was known
for her lightheartedness and "vivacity."[1] But the adolescent
patterns set in unhappiness were the important ones for her
future, and indeed these are the clearest in the evidence at
hand.

From her tenth to her fifteenth year Mary's father owned
and worked one farm, which was close outside Beverley in

---

[1] Cameron, ed., *Shelley and His Circle*, II, "Appendix," 982, 964, 967.

Yorkshire (it was the longest period Mary lived in one spot, not only in her youth but in her whole life). Beverley was a charming old town and around it was lovely countryside, both of which she explored and loved. There is a familiar figure in the teen-age girl who wandered her "favourite walks" around the farm and through the town, or at any rate, one not unlike that caught in Simone de Beauvoir's classic sketch: "While the adolescent boy makes his way actively toward adulthood, the young girl awaits the opening of this new, unforeseeable period. . . . [Her] youth is consumed in waiting . . . a time of transition. . . . She is busy, but she *does* nothing; because she does nothing, she *has* nothing, she *is* nothing. She must fill this void with play-acting and falsification." And, because "she does not act, she observes, she feels, she records . . . her destiny is outside her, scattered in cities already built, on the faces of men already marked by life; she makes contact, she relishes with passion and yet in a manner more detached, more free, than that of a young man."[2]

Mary got all her formal education at a day school in Beverley, where she learned at least the pleasures of "wide reading." She read poetry, we know, for when a friend, Jane Arden, was away visiting in neighboring Hull, Mary wrote her letters that carefully and fashionably used copied lines as emphasis of her points, but at anything else (girlish romances, *Roxana*, Fielding, Richardson, devotional literature?) we can only guess. The letters to Jane Arden are very much those of a fourteen-year-old: their tone is at once that of a "genteel" grown-up note ("Dear Miss Arden/ According to my promise I sit down to write to you") and the exuberant rattling of the child ("P.S. Pray write soon—I have a hundred things to add, but can't get time for my Mama is calling me, so shall reserve them for another letter"). They demonstrate, for one thing, that Mary was much involved in the social rounds of her friends (Miss G____, Miss R____, Miss C____), and, for another, that the shakiness of grammar and punctuation that

[2] Beauvoir, *Second Sex*, pp. 328, 357, 361.

marked her writing all her life had something to do with the day school instruction in Beverley.[3]

Perhaps the adolescent Mary was "freer" than her brother Edward, who was off mastering the law, free because as a girl she had no structured role in society and no pressure to learn anything very precisely, free to poke through the lanes and alleys of her environment, free to gossip and day-dream and experiment with poses, to be even—in Beauvoir's words— a "sovereign subject" of Nature, to see in it the "reflection of the solitude of her soul."[4] And yet, observe in the description of the fictional Mary's absorption with nature the revelation of the limits of her freedom:

Sublime ideas filled her young mind—always connected with devotional sentiments; extemporary effusions of gratitude, and rhapsodies of praise would burst often from her, when she listened to the birds, or pursued the deer. She would gaze on the moon, and ramble through the gloomy path, observing the various shapes the clouds assumed, and listen to the sea that was not far distant. The wandering spirits, which she imagined inhabited every part of nature, were her constant friends and confidants. She began to consider the Great First Cause, formed just notions of his attributes, and, in particular, dwelt on wisdom and goodness. Could she have loved her father and mother, had they returned her affection, she would not so soon, perhaps, have sought out a new world.[5]

"Could she have loved her father and mother, had they returned her affection, she would not so soon, perhaps, have sought out a new world"—neither "empty" nor "unlimited" in the fleeting time of girlhood, Mary carried dominating emotional burdens. That they filled her relations with her parents we know; what is impressive here is their intrusion into her adolescent social contacts. She wrote, before her family moved away from Beverley, seven letters to Jane Arden. Three of them were written after Jane returned from Hull with a

[3] Cameron, ed., *Shelley and His Circle*, II, 944, 946, 950–954.
[4] Beauvoir, *Second Sex*, p. 363.
[5] Wollstonecraft, *Mary*, pp. 12–13.

houseguest, a Miss C———, and have to do with Mary's possessive pout that she was being excluded by the girl she regarded
as her dearest friend. In the first letter she was angry and
unhappy but not quite ready to explain herself:

Miss A._____ Your behaviour at Miss J_____'s hurt me ex-
tremely, and your not answering my letter shews that you set little
value on my friendship. —If you had sent to ask me, I should have
gone to the play, but none of you seemed to want my company. —I
have two favors to beg, the one is that you will send me all my
letters; —the other that you will never mention some things
which I have told you. To avoid idle tell-tale, we may visit
ceremoniously, and to keep up appearances, may whisper, when
we have nothing to say: —the beaux whisper insignificantly,
and nod without meaning. —I beg you will take the trouble to
bring the letters yourself, or give them to my sister Betsy. —You
never called yesterday; if you wish to be on the least friendly
footing, you will call this morning. —If you think it worth while,
send an answer by my sister.[6]

An adolescent tempest in a teapot, with its childish anger and
half-grown threats and pleadings? The next letter, in which
Mary told Jane the real problem, was the first of a kind she
would write in similar emotional moments all her life (the last
to William Godwin only weeks before her death):

Miss Arden. —Before I begin I beg pardon for the freedom of
my style. —If I did not love you I should not write so; —I have a
heart that scorns disguise, and a countenance which will not
dissemble: —I have formed romantic notions of friendship. —I
have been once disappointed: —I think if I am a second time I
shall only want some infidelity in a love affair, to qualify me for
an old maid, as then I shall have no idea of either of them. —I am
a little singular in my thoughts of love and friendship; I must
have the first place or none. —I own your behaviour is more
according to the opinion of the world, but I would break such
narrow bounds. —I will give you my reasons for what I say;
—since Miss C_____ has been here you have behaved in the coolest

[6] Cameron, ed., *Shelley and His Circle*, II, 954-955.

manner. —I once hoped our friendship was built on a permanent foundation: —We have all our failings—I have more than usual, but I thought you might mildly have corrected me as I always loved you with true sisterly affection. If I had found any faults I should have told you but a lady possessed of so many accomplishments as Miss A_____ cannot want for admirers, and who has so many friends cannot find any loss in your humble Servant. —I would not have seen it, but your behaviour the other night I cannot pass over; —when I spoke of sitting with you at Church you made an objection, because I and your sister quarrelled; —I did not think a little raillery would have been taken in such a manner, or that you would have insinuated, that I dared to have prophaned so sacred a place with idle chit-chat.

I once thought myself worthy of your friendship; —I thank you for bringing me to a right sense of myself. —When I have been at your house with Miss J_____ the greatest respect has been paid to her; every thing handed to her first; —in short, as if she were a superior being. —Your Mama too behaved with more politeness to her.

I am much obliged to your Papa and Mama and desire you will give them my complimentary thanks, and as I have spent many happy hours in your company, shall always have the sincerest esteem for Miss A_____. —There is no accounting for the imbecility of human nature. —I might misconstrue your behaviour, but what I have written flows spontaneously from my pen and this I am sure, I only desire to be done by as I do; —I shall expect a written answer to this,—

and am yours
M. W.

Don't tell C_____ to you I have told all my failings; —I would not be so mean as to shew only the bright side of the picture; —I have reason to think you have not been so ingenuous to me. —I cannot bear the reflection that when Miss R_____ comes I should have less of your company. —After seeing you yesterday, I thought not to have sent this—(but you desire it) for to see you and be angry, is not in my power. —I long for a walk in my darling Westwood. Adieu.

Mary Wollstonecraft.[7]

[7] *Ibid.*, pp. 955–956.

That this letter is one of the very few existing from Mary's girlhood is either a remarkable accident or terribly significant. It is a total exposure—of her ego problem, of her desperate need to be "first" in the affections of any chosen love-object, yet of the side of her that was too powerful to retreat when rebuffed, though she tried to do so, into injured silence and isolated hostility.

The issue of Miss C—— passed; Mary's third and final letter on the quarrel was part apology and part reiteration of her unhappiness ("Love and Jealousy are twins," she told Jane), but the hurt was less acute. One guesses that Jane was both annoyed and flattered by Mary's behavior, but primarily willing to forget it.[8] The problem, though, did not go away. She would have first place or none, Mary had written; even before the Jane incident she felt she had been "once disappointed" in friendship, and was half-preparing herself for the "infidelity in a love affair" that would qualify her for an "old maid." If such were Mary's experience and expectations in love and friendship (one remembers with difficulty that she was just fourteen years old), it is not surprising that she looked elsewhere for more rewarding gratifications—religion, for example.

The adult Mary would have for the religious faith she stubbornly preserved even as an enlightened radical a breath-takingly rational explanation: in an angry moment with Godwin she wrote him, "how can you blame me for taken [*sic*] refuge in the idea of a God, when I despair of finding sincerity on earth?"[9] "Could she have loved her father and mother, had they returned her affection . . ."—the adolescent Mary who was unappreciated and unloved at home, denied total friendship by Jane Arden and others, would find consolation and eternal love in the arms of the universal Father, and in adoration of Him find an acceptable outlet for her intense feelings and emotions. The heroine of *Mary* got her deepest adolescent

[8] *Ibid.*, pp. 956–958.
[9] Ralph M. Wardle, ed., *Godwin and Mary: Letters of William Godwin and Mary Wollstonecraft* (Lawrence, Kan., 1966), p. 111.

satisfaction in religious ecstasy. Mary wrote of her "enthusias-
tic sentiments of devotion at this period," of "violent," "trembling" emotions on her confirmation day, and of the "many
nights she sat up . . . conversing with the Author of Nature,
making verses, and singing hymns of her own composing."[10] In
thus communicating with God there was no harsh criticism, no
rejection: the fictional Mary "thought that only an infinite
being could fill the human soul, and that when other objects
were followed as a means of happiness, the delusion led to
misery, the consequence of disappointment."[11]

The story in *Mary* is explicit on the concomitant satisfactions of this adolescent religiosity. Consoled in the bosom of
the Lord, the young heroine both lives His word and assures
His continuing love by "usefulness," by charitable work and
benevolence for the poor and the needy. Analyzing her fictional shadow, author Mary proposed that caring for others,
being involved in the distress of others, "carried her out of
herself."[12] The transparency of the youthful egoism is striking:
what is obvious is that in the act of "benevolence [that] knew
no bounds" she was self-consciously watching herself, delighted with the spectacle of herself Being Benevolent. Listen
to the words of this account in the novel:

At a little distance . . . were the huts of a few poor fishermen,
who supported their numerous children by their precarious labour. In these little huts she frequently rested, and denied herself
every childish gratification, in order to relieve the necessities of
the inhabitants. Her heart yearned for them, and would dance
with joy when she had relieved their wants, or afforded them
pleasure . . . and she rested not till she had relieved or comforted
them. The warmth of her compassion often made her so diligent,
that many things occurred to her, which might have escaped a less
interested observer.

In these pursuits she learned the luxury of doing good; and the
sweet tears of benevolence frequently moistened her eyes, and
gave them a sparkle which, exclusive of that they had not.[13]

[10] Wollstonecraft, *Mary*, p. 28.     [11] *Ibid.*     [12] *Ibid.*, p. 26.
[13] *Ibid.*, pp. 25–26.

One is more than ever grateful for the naiveté of *Mary* in so obligingly providing a psychology of charitable activities. But the thoughts and words—and values—of the passage above are more than an amusingly earnest adolescent search for transcendence in the spiritual. One should keep in mind that the book was written when Mary was twenty-seven years old. The complex revealed here—Mary's piety, her self-conscious self-righteousness (shot through with self-pity)—was a portentous construction. Perhaps in its teen-age inception it meant this: within her project of being useful and thereby winning heavenly love and approval, she was working hard for rewards from material deities. Perhaps her adolescent religiosity was a concession to her mother, and a parody of what she felt to be her mother's response to life. Thus, rebuffed in her childish egoism, half-conditioned to distrust her passionately willful self—that unlovable, certainly pain-creating part of herself—the young Mary was preparing to reproduce, in her own formidably energetic way, her mother's example of withdrawal and self-abnegation, of passive acceptance of life's destiny. She too would be a noble sufferer, bowing before God's will and the trials of a life in which personal happiness and fulfillment were not part of a heavenly plan; indeed, with a higher morality than her mother's, she would submerge herself in the happiness of others. Piety and devotion and self-sacrifice to the welfare of others, which not so incidentally put her into situations in which she was both safe and in control, with "inferiors" who were on the defensive of gratitude and not apt to judge or reject their benefactress—it was a neat compromise. It was also a strange, hybrid identity-process, this active creation of passivity.

## II

When she was about sixteen, Mary met Frances (Fanny) Blood, a girl two years older than she, with whom she "contracted a friendship so fervent, as for years to have constituted the ruling passion of her mind."[14] "Fervent," "passionate," those words so odd amidst Godwin's cool prose, are an appropriate introduction to the key relationship of Mary's adolescence and young womanhood. Fanny would be the standard by which Mary measured her ego, the foil to the working out—in a peculiar and partial way—of her problems of love and rejection, and finally the dependent to be treasured and cared for in weakness and need.

Here again Godwin's *Memoirs* and the novel *Mary*—the latter written explicitly as a memorial to Mary's friendship with Fanny—carry the story; the narrative of the *Memoirs* is heavy with what could only be Mary's later perceptions of the relationship, while that of the novel adds convincingly closer details.

In the first excitement of finding a friend, Mary, "still a wild, but animated and aspiring girl of sixteen,"[15] thought Fanny a model of absolute perfection. She saw her initially in a Werther-like scene, Fanny as Lotte, lovingly attending her younger brothers and sisters in the Blood home. Fanny was a slim, composed, wholly feminine young lady, talented with needle, pen, and even drawing materials; indeed, she had sold some of her sketches commercially. Equally interesting, she was in love, with a young man named Hugh Skeys, with whom she was contemplating marriage. Mary was charmed, fascinated, and envious; her feelings, Godwin says, were a mixture of "inferiority and reverence."[16] Fanny lived in the south of London in Newington Butts, and the Wollstonecrafts, finished with Yorkshire farming, were briefly in Hoxton, so that the girls saw one another only rarely. They corresponded though, and the correspondence was both enlightening and humiliating for Mary; she was "abashed" to discover that Fanny's letters were "better spelt and better indited" than her own, and to realize that she had "hitherto paid but a superficial attention to literature," that she had not before "thought of writing as an art."[17] But she was willing to learn from Fanny—in fact, she

---

[14] Godwin, *Memoirs*, p. 18.     [15] *Ibid.*, p. 20.     [16] *Ibid.*
[17] *Ibid.*

was challenged: "Her ambition to excel was now awakened, and she applied herself with passion and earnestness. Fanny undertook to be her instructor; and, so far as related to accuracy and method, her lessons were given with considerable skill."[18]

Godwin concentrated here on what interested him, that is, Fanny's influence in helping Mary over some of the rough spots of an education that must have been indifferent at best. In *Mary* the emphasis is on different, more subtle aspects of the relationship. The novel makes explicit, for example, the heavy demands that Mary put on her new friend (whose fictional name is Ann). When the girls meet, the heroine, sensitive, intelligent, unloved Mary, is in her mid-teens, and adjusting to the reality that consolation in life lay only in her communion with God-in-Nature and in usefulness to God's creatures. Friendship with Ann is an exhilaration she has never known, its adolescent intensity a compensation for all the deprivation of her past. When she was with Ann "she felt less pain on account of her mother's partiality to her brother, as she hoped now to experience the pleasures of being beloved. . . ." But, the passage goes on, "this hope led her into new sorrows, and as usual paved the way for disappointment."[19] In short, Mary expected Fanny to be not only friend and adolescent confidante but mother as well, and to give her total attention and love; it was an expectation that poor Fanny, who had problems and inadequacies of her own, was quite incapable of satisfying.

Fanny's chief problem was her love for Hugh Skeys, whose reluctance to pursue courtship was her not-so-secret grief. It was her pining for the indecisive Skeys, indeed her absorption with him, that so hurt Mary, caused her sorrow and disappointment—"as usual." In the novel she explained her feelings in these revealing words:

When her friend was all the world to her, she found she was not as necessary to her happiness; and her delicate mind could not

---

[18] *Ibid.*      [19] Wollstonecraft, *Mary*, p. 21.

bear to obtrude her affection, or receive love as an alms, the offspring of pity. Very frequently has she run to her with delight, and not perceiving any thing of the same kind in Ann's countenance, she has shrunk back; and, falling from one extreme into the other, instead of a warm greeting that was just slipping from her tongue, her expression seemed to be dictated by the most chilling insensibility.[20]

The scene was one that Mary must have played over and over with her mother; certainly it was a memory and a behavior pattern that remained with her always. (Years after her early relations with Fanny she wrote this in a letter to Gilbert Imlay: "One thing you mistake in my character, and imagine that to be coldness which is just the contrary. For, when I am hurt by the person most dear to me, I must let out a whole torrent of emotions, in which tenderness would be uppermost, or stifle them altogether; and it appears to me almost a duty to stifle them, when I imagine *that I am treated with coldness.*")[21] Fanny's inability to enter an exclusive relationship, her elusiveness at being possessed, triggered Mary's insecurities, set in motion first her suspiciousness, then stiff, retaliatory pride. If Fanny loved someone else, how could she love Mary? To Mary it was that simple, as was her reaction: she would not "obtrude her affection" and in return "receive love as an alms"; she would not be caught in emotional imbalance, in the ultimate humiliation that was love as "pity."

Yet—and this is the subsequent significant point—Mary found a way to handle the old emotional syndrome that she had carried over into her love for Fanny Blood. That way was through the newly articulated identity of Mary the sympathizer, Mary the benefactress of the unfortunate of her world. Immediately following the description of the heroine Mary shrinking back from Ann's perceived indifference and of her substitution of the "most chilling insensibility" for her real warmth and pleasure at seeing her friend, came these words:

[20] *Ibid.*, pp. 21–22.
[21] Ingpen, ed., *Letters to Imlay*, XII (Mary's emphasis).

Mary "would then imagine that [Ann] looked sickly or unhappy, and then all her tenderness would return like a torrent,
and bear away all reflection. In this manner was her sensibility
called forth. . . ."[22] And in truth Fanny was someone to feel
sympathy for: not only did she sigh for unrequited love, but
she was frail and consumptive, and bored and unhappy in a
family atmosphere so harmonious that she considered it the
essence of dullness. Concentrating on these things, Mary could
right the balance of the relationship and in fact take the upper
hand as the person absolutely essential to Fanny's emotional
well-being.

"I think," Mary wrote in 1785—she was in her twenties—"I
love most people best when they are in adversity, for pity is
one of my prevailing passions."[23] The relationship with Fanny
Blood was the first fully developed demonstration of that quite
accurate self-characterization. Mary's love for Fanny reached a
"fervent" pitch once she had established the friendship on her
own terms. She loved Ann, ran the narrative in *Mary*, "better
than any one in the world—to snatch her from the very jaws
of destruction—she would have encountered a lion. To have
this friend constantly with her; to make her mind easy with
respect to her family, would it not be superlative bliss?"[24] And
the intensification of her love was paralleled by the transition
of feelings from the original admiration, "reverence," to pity,
and on to something akin to contempt. For one thing, from
being her pupil Mary travelled rapidly to this kind of judgment of Fanny's intellectual gifts: "In every thing it was not
the great, but the beautiful, or the pretty, that caught her
attention. And in composition, the polish of style, and harmony of numbers, interested her much more than the flights of
genius, or abstracted speculations. She often wondered at the
books Mary chose, who, though she had a lively imagination
would frequently study authors whose works were addressed
to the understanding. This liking taught [Mary] to arrange her

[22] Wollstonecraft, *Mary*, p. 22.
[23] Letter to George Blood, quoted in Paul, *Godwin*, I, 175.
[24] Wollstonecraft, *Mary*, p. 39.

thoughts, and argue with herself, even when under the influence of the most violent passions."[25] Or, mixed with compassion for Fanny's bad luck with the reluctant Mr. Skeys was this hard evaluation: "She was timid and irresolute, and rather fond of dissipation; grief only had power to make her reflect [rather than act as, no doubt, Mary would in her position]."[26] By the time Godwin got to direct comparison of Mary and Fanny, the contrast is almost brutal: "Whatever Mary undertook, she perhaps in all instances accomplished; and, to her lofty spirit, scarcely anything she desired, appeared hard to perform. Fanny, on the contrary, was a woman of a timid and irresolute nature, accustomed to yield to difficulties, and probably priding herself in this morbid softness of her temper."[27] Fanny's timidity, her indecisiveness, her "morbid softness" (reminiscent of Elizabeth Wollstonecraft?)—these perceived qualities were the secret of her appeal for Mary. Pity was indeed one of Mary's "prevailing passions"; it was her strongest defense, the mechanism by which she held the upper hand in that thing of pain and uncertainty she knew as love.

[25] *Ibid.*, p. 35.     [26] *Ibid.*     [27] Godwin, *Memoirs*, p. 30.

# Chapter Three

# THE DEPENDENT SPINSTER

. . . I am persuaded misfortunes are of the greatest
service, as they set things in the light they ought to be
viewed in and give those who are tried by them a
kind of early old age.

Letter to Jane Arden

. . . It is a most unfortunate condition to be in, to feel
oneself passive and dependent at the age of hope and
ambition, at the age when the will to live and to make
a place in the world is running strong.

*The Second Sex*

*b*y her eighteenth year Mary, like Fanny, was chaf-
ing at her dependence upon her parents, though
unlike Fanny she had harsh reasons to be unhappy. Her home was intolerable to her now, perhaps had
been so since the last year in Beverley. Evidently her father's
habits and disposition, and his mismanagement of his estate,
had been gossip items there: letters written to Jane Arden after
Mary left home assume the knowledge that Edward John's
"violent temper and extravagant turn of mind" had made the
whole family miserable. In fact, Mary carried a grievance
against the "good folks of Beverley" who "did not scruple to
prognosticate the ruin" of the Wollstonecrafts, though she had
to admit that her father's behavior had "justified them for so
doing."[1] In desperate moves to recoup his dwindling inheritance the father took them, within three years, to Hoxton, to
Wales, and back to London, his temper all the while growing
more "ungovernable." Finally, his affairs were in such a mess

[1] Cameron, ed., *Shelley and His Circle*, II, 965.

that he dipped into the "fortune" that had been settled on the children; Mary was so disgusted with him and his "misconduct," so anxious to get out unencumbered, that she "very readily gave up" her portion.[2]

At nineteen, then, Mary had had enough. Somehow dealing with her mother's and probably her sisters' entreaties to remain, she went out into the world, alone and unsupported, to make her own way. Nineteen—she was half child, half woman: the child running away from a loveless home, taking with her all unresolved her childish problems (and looking back over her shoulder to watch the effects of her departure on her parents), but a young woman too, with a realistic sense of her limits. A girl in her position might have gone into one of the few trades open to women, might have prepared to become, say, a milliner, and work toward an independence in that line. That "Mary the milliner" even sounds ridiculous is a statement of the social route the Wollstonecrafts had taken, away from London trade and toward the status of the lesser gentry. One can be sure that the youthful Mary (and in her later fiction she would refer to the trades as "degrading to a gentlewoman")[3] did not stop to consider this kind of working woman's career. Or she might have looked for a husband. Not even Mary was unaware of the supreme value—the only value —in the feminine middle-class code that marriage was. True, with their disappearing assets and a social position that had never been more than marginal, the Wollstonecrafts were not a first family in the marriage market (in Mary's fiction her heroines are naturally enmeshed in ugly, commercialized, parent-arranged marital deals, in plots so stiffly artificial that she must have gotten them from reading third-rate Richardson rather than experience). Still, sister Eliza—she was, Mary said, the "handsome" one of the family[4]—would soon take marriage as a way out and presumably Mary might have at least thought of doing the same. But this was becoming her area of flat dogma-

---

[2] *Ibid.*, pp. 966, 965.        [3] Godwin, *Posthumous Works, Maria*, II, 17.
[4] Cameron, ed., *Shelley and His Circle*, II, 966.

tism: she had decided at fifteen, she later told Godwin, never to marry for "interested motives," nor to endure a "life of dependence,"[5] and whatever ugliness she had witnessed or experienced with her parents in the intervening years, by nineteen she was on the way to absolute aversion to the institution. The only "choice" she had, then, was that respectable employment for the inexperienced and indifferently educated young spinster lumped under teaching, child care, and companionship to the wealthy. She took a job as companion to a Mrs. Dawson, who lived in plush retirement in Bath, the "widow of an opulent tradesman of the city of London," and a lady known as having "great peculiarity of temper."[6] It was not an appealing plan, but it was all she had.

Mary spent two years as a companion, and hated it bitterly. A more compliant and self-satisfied young female might have pronounced the position quite pleasant. Mrs. Dawson was neither so formidable nor so dreary as her reputation promised; Mary had to admit that she had a "very good understanding," and since she had seen a "great deal of the world" her conversation was interesting and instructive to her young companion.[7] And living by the Dawson standards might have delighted a typical girl: Bath was at the peak of its magnificence, a city of "incomparable beauties" and "noble effects,"[8] the grace and elegance and splendor of its public buildings and private homes consonant with its place as a mandatory "season" resort of the English social elites. They vacationed in Southampton—Mary was advised there to "bathe in the Sea"—and at Windsor, the "gayest of all gay places," where she could watch "all the damsels set their caps" for the Prince of Wales.[9] Proximity to the wealthy, the leisured, the fashionable, the famous—it should have been exciting, or at the very least, distracting.

[5] Wardle, ed., *Godwin and Mary*, p. 28.

[6] Godwin, *Memoirs*, p. 22 fn.

[7] Cameron, ed., *Shelley and His Circle*, II, 968.

[8] Rev. S. Shaw, *A Tour to the West of England in 1788* (London, 1789), pp. 285, 289.

[9] Cameron, ed., *Shelley and His Circle*, II, 967, 971.

But Mary was determined to be misanthropic. There was no solution for her basic complaint: she found her work unendurable, as nasty a kind of servitude as she had had at home. To be utterly "dependant [*sic*] on the caprice of a fellow-creature," she would later write, meant frustration and impotence, "hours of anguish" in a situation structured so that one was "above the servants, yet considered by them as a spy, and ever reminded of . . . inferiority when in conversation with the superiors."[10] "Penance and mortification" indeed was this effort to earn her living; "necessity not choice ties me to it," Mary wrote in a letter to Jane Arden: "if I was to follow the bent of my inclination I sho[uld] haste away."[11]

And thus she was not to be distracted by the sights of the residential spas of the rich. She wrote letters to Jane Arden—the only direct record of her period of employment—in which she occasionally tried to be an entertaining correspondent, but the persistent tone is depression and introspective gloom. Southampton, she wrote, was "a very pleasant place in every sense of the word," and Bath was "agreeable," though in its "natural beauties" much "inferior" to Wales. Windsor was "charming," and especially delightful in its surrounding forest retreats, but "too gay," with nothing but "dress and amusements . . . going forward" (this was her criticism of Bath too, where she was oppressed by "balls & plays without end or number").[12] "To say the truth," she told Jane, "I am very indifferent to the opinion of the world in general;—I wish to retire as much from it as possible—I am particularly sick of genteel life, as it is called;—the unmeaning civilities that I see every day practiced don't agree with my temper;—I long for a little sincerity, and look forward with pleasure to the time when I shall lay aside all restraint."[13]

Most of the time Mary saw nothing at all to look forward to with pleasure. She was a "spectator" of life, she told Jane; mixing little with the world and "slower than ever in forming

[10] Wollstonecraft, *Thoughts on the Education of Daughters*, pp. 71, 70.
[11] Cameron, ed., *Shelley and His Circle*, II, 970.
[12] *Ibid.*, pp. 968, 977, 975, 971.     [13] *Ibid.*, p. 975.

friendships," she was a solitary whose favorite refuge in Windsor was the cathedral, where she was "very fond of the Service."[14] Now she was twenty years old and becoming a philosopher of martyred resignation. "Pain and disappointment" had been her lot since she left Beverley; her health was "ruined," her "spirits broken," and she had a "constant pain" in her side that was "daily gaining ground."[15] But, she said,

I do not however repine at the dispensations of Providence, for my philosophy, as well as my religion will ever teach me to look on misfortunes as blessings, which like a bitter potion is disagreeable to the palate tho' 'tis grateful to the Stomach—I hope mine have not been thrown away on me, but that I am both the wiser, and better for them. . . . Young people generally set out with romantic and sanguine hopes of happiness, and must receive a great many stings before they are convinced of their mistake, and that they are pursuing a mere phantom; an empty name.[16]

Again and again she restated her "philosophy," somehow comforted by the words: "Reason as well as religion convinces me all has happened for the best.—This is an old worn-out maxim, but it is not the less true for, I am persuaded misfortunes are of the greatest service, as they set things in the light they ought to be viewed in and give those who are tried by them a kind of early old age."[17] With such thoughts to give her strength, she would struggle to attain a "cheerful settled frame of mind" in waiting for "that abode of peace" of a "better world."[18]

But by her second year with Mrs. Dawson, the philosopher of resignation was planning quite practically for her immediate future. She had a week's vacation to visit Fanny Blood in London, and after her return she wrote to Jane Arden that the next meeting with Fanny would be "for a longer continuance." She was determined, she said, to let nothing interfere with a decision she had come to during her vacation, and that was to live with Fanny. It was life-planning she was doing, for

[14] *Ibid.*, pp. 975, 971, 970, 977.  [15] *Ibid.*, pp. 964–965.
[16] *Ibid.*, p. 965.  [17] *Ibid.*, p. 968.  [18] *Ibid.*, pp. 967, 975.

she added, "I know this resolution may appear a little extraordinary, but in forming it I follow the dictates of reason as well as the bent of my inclinations; for tho' I am willing to do what good I can in my generation, yet on many accounts I am averse to any matrimonial tie. . . ."[19] Dependent spinsterhood was the condition she had resolved to escape from; somehow in a life with Fanny she would achieve the opposite kind. In this letter, not so incidentally, Mary referred to a plan of Jane Arden's to open a boarding school for young ladies: "I have ever approved of your plan . . . let not some small difficulties intimidate you, I beseech you;—struggle with any obstacles rather than go into a state of dependance [sic]: —I speak feelingly. —I have felt the weight, and wo[uld] have you by all means avoid it."[20]

The idea of living with Fanny—it "gladdens my heart," Mary told Jane Arden, and "you know not how I love her"[21] —was the one bright hope in the gloom and pessimism of the last year with Mrs. Dawson. Dependent spinsterhood ended, however, not with resolution but necessity: Mary was called home because of her mother's fatal illness, though Elizabeth Wollstonecraft was a long time dying. Mary took over total direction of the household and did all the nursing of the patient, during months that should have brought a satiation of "usefulness" and caring for the unfortunate. It was a crucial, pivotal period for Mary. Through her exhaustion and sorrow she must have gotten exquisite pleasure—as she had once gotten "exquisite pain"—from her mother in those months, pleasure from being and doing the things Elizabeth approved of, from demonstrating her sense of duty and responsibility, from giving the dying woman not only efficient but patient and tender care. Her old ambivalence toward her mother, her memories of coldness and indifference, could be wiped out by the fact of her own controlling and necessary position, by pity for her mother's condition, by her self-righteous awareness of her value and performance. The final, the climactic, scene

[19] *Ibid.*, pp. 976–977.     [20] *Ibid.*, p. 976.     [21] *Ibid.*, p. 979.

of the death of the mother is a dramatic moment in both of Mary's novels, *Mary* and *Maria*. In the former, the mother on her deathbed asks the daughter's forgiveness for the harshness she had used with her; in *Maria* she begs the daughter to take care of the younger children, to "be a mother" to them.[22]

With her mother's death Mary was free, of both Mrs. Dawson and home. There is no mention of an even fleeting thought of returning to her job, and the paternal roof fast became so distasteful—as though part of a script, Edward John installed his mistress as housekeeper—that Mary's younger sisters prepared to leave too, Everina to keep house for elder brother Edward, for some time established as a London attorney, and Eliza in marriage to a Mr. Bishop. Nothing prevented Mary from going to Fanny Blood and independent spinsterhood, and she did so with dispatch.

Of her thoughts as she travelled the distance to Walham Green, south of London, or as she settled in with the Bloods, we have no idea. She wrote two last letters to Jane Arden after she left home, the first relating the facts of her mother's death, the second a gratuitous blast against marriage, particularly so because it was occasioned by news of the wedding of Jane's sister. These were Mary's congratulatory reflections:

I was just going to desire you to wish her joy (to use the common phrase) but I am afraid my good wishes might be unseasonable, as I find by the date of your letter that the honey moon, and the next moon too must be almost over——The joy, and all that, is certainly over by this time, and all the raptures have subsided, and the dear hurry of visiting and figuring away as a bride, and all the rest of the delights of matrimony are past and gone and have left no traces behind them, except disgust:—I hope I am mistaken, but this is the fate of most married pairs.—Solomon says "there is nothing new under the sun" for which reason I will not marry, for I dont want to be tied to this nasty world, and old maids are of so little consequence—that "let them live or die, nobody will laugh or cry."—It is a happy thing to be a mere blank, and to be

[22] Wollstonecraft, *Mary*, p. 40; Godwin, *Posthumous Works*, *Maria*, I, 174.

able to pursue one's own whims, where they lead, without having a husband and half a hundred children at hand to teaze and controul a poor woman who wishes to be free. . . .[23]

("Ah, poor Mary," perhaps Jane Arden mused to herself. It was the last time she would hear from her friend of Beverley school-days.)

So Mary was determined to be an inconsequential old maid, but what of her immediate and practical activity? She had decided, Godwin said, to give up adventures for herself alone: leaving home and family for a job with Mrs. Dawson had been mere "solitary gratification," an attempt to remove "personal vexations," and consequently a selfish and self-centered act.[24] What would be an unselfish act? To put her benevolent self at the service of her family and friends? To insure that although Elizabeth Wollstonecraft was dead, she would live on in her eldest daughter? To lose her selfish self and find her life's role in the essential task of assisting the weak and improvident of her circle? We have no insight into Mary's consciousness after her mother died. But we do know what she did in the next few years: she became in fact surrogate-mother not only to her younger brothers and sisters but to the Blood family as well, and (as the independent spinster, everybody's old maid aunt) would have taken in, one feels, any other stray, indecisive soul who might have sought refuge beneath her protective, if odd, maternal wing.

[23] Cameron, ed., *Shelley and His Circle*, II, 983.
[24] Godwin, *Memoirs*, p. 25.

MARY WOLLSTONECRAFT

*Courtesy of the National Portrait Gallery, London*

WILLIAM GODWIN

*Courtesy of the British Museum*

# Chapter Four

# THE INDEPENDENT SPINSTER

---

... Universal Benevolence is the first duty, and we
should be careful not to let any passion ... prevent
our practicing it.

*Thoughts on the Education of Daughters*

... for the young woman ... there is a contradiction between her status as a real human being and her
vocation as a female.... Her spontaneous tendency is
to regard herself as the essential: how can she make up
her mind to become the inessential? ... [She] reacts
variably to this situation according to her earlier
tendencies ... she may have taken on, as "little
mother," a taste for authority which leads her to rebel
against the masculine yoke: she is ready to found a
matriarchate but not to become an erotic object and a
servant.

*The Second Sex*

---

*M*ARY arrived at the Blood home in Walham Green
in 1781 (aftermath of the Gordon Riots, shouts for
reform of Parliament, end of the war in the American colonies? Mary was oblivious to it all). She made herself
useful—restlessly, perhaps—helping with the needlework that
was Mrs. Blood's genteel but quite essential occupation. The
Bloods were respectable but poor, not least because Mr. Blood
was a "drunken spendthrift"[1]—another unfortunate male
model for Mary, though Blood, unlike her father, was a gentle
inebriate. During Mary's visit the family's financial distress was
becoming desperation, a compound of Blood's proclivities and

---

[1] Paul, *Godwin*, I, 165.

the effects of war-time inflation and taxation, and Mary surely did all she could to help. But a good guess is that she was thinking about other things too, plans to take care of sister Everina, whose presence in his home Edward did not welcome, or to help sister Eliza, married to her Mr. Bishop; and surely she was thinking about Fanny, talented, dreamy, and bored, wanting above all, as she told Mary in confidence, "a home of her own."[2]

The first of Mary's projects as family director was so fantastic that it might well be a bit of Gothic drama. Late in 1782 she was called to the bedside of her sister Eliza, who was ill after the birth of a baby (a girl, who was named Mary). Eliza's postnatal difficulties were apparently psychological—perhaps she was high-strung, prone to hysteria—and therefore mysteriously dreadful to Mary. In a letter to Everina (and Mary's letters are the only source of information on the episode) soon after her arrival, Mary described their sister's symptoms:

I cannot yet give any certain account of Bess, or form a rational conjecture with respect to the termination of her disorder. She has not had a violent fit of frenzy since I saw you, but her mind is in a most unsettled state, and attending to the constant fluctuation of it is far more harassing than the watching those raving fits that had not the least tincture of reason. Her ideas are all disjointed, and a number of wild whims float on her imagination, and fall from her unconnectedly, something like strange dreams when judgment sleeps, and fancy sports at a fine rate. Don't smile at my language, for I am so constantly forced to observe her—lest she run into mischief—that my thoughts continually turn on the unaccountable wanderings of her mind. She seems to think she has been very ill used, and, in short, till I see some more favourable symptoms I shall only suppose that her malady has assumed a new and more distressing appearance.[3]

If Eliza had indeed been "ill used" in her marriage, and that was Mary's implication, she had entered her complaint with the right person. Mary had no trouble fixing on Bishop as the cause of her sister's disintegration, and once she had made that

[2] Godwin, *Memoirs*, p. 31.    [3] Paul, *Godwin*, I, 166.

identification she was not likely to let it go, though her readers might not be automatically convinced of his exclusive guilt. Even she seemed ambivalent in discussing Bishop, a young man who was, in a friend's words, "either a lion or a spaniel": in one letter she admitted that she could not help pitying him, and in another her heart was "almost broken" in listening to him "reason the case."[4] Still, she judged, "misery must be his portion at any rate till he alters himself, and that would be a miracle." If that did not settle poor Bishop, she added, "May my habitation never be fixed among the tribe that can't look beyond the present gratification. . . ."[5]

So a month after she had arrived, Mary decided firmly that Eliza's health and sanity depended on leaving her husband. She wrote to Everina:

I don't know what to do. Poor Eliza's situation almost turns my brain. I can't stay and see this continual misery, and to leave her to bear it by herself without any one to comfort her, is still more distressing. I would do anything to rescue her from her present situation. My head is quite confused with thus being to so little purpose. In this case something desperate must be determined on. Do you think Edward will receive her? [Edward would *not* receive her.] Do speak to him; or if you imagine that I should have more influence on his mind, I will contrive to see you, but you must caution him against expostulating with or even mentioning the affair to Bishop, for it would only put him on his guard, and we should have a storm to encounter that I tremble to think of. I am convinced that this is the only expedient to save Bess, and she declares she had rather be a teacher than stay here. . . .

To be at Edward's is not desirable, but of the two evils she must choose the least . . . I tell you she will soon be deprived of reason. B. cannot behave properly, and those who would attempt to reason with him must be mad, or have very little observation. Those who would save Bess must act and not talk.[6]

"Those who would save Bess must act and not talk"—Mary's resolution was taking shape. One day in January, 1783, while

---

[4] *Ibid.*, pp. 167–168.    [5] *Ibid.*, p. 168.    [6] *Ibid.*, pp. 167–168.

Bishop was out of the house, she spirited Eliza away—without baby Mary—took two carriages "to prevent his tracing us," and holed up as a "Miss Johnston and Mrs. Dodds" in a room "opposite the Mermaid, Church St., Hackney."[7] The daring and danger of the scheme shook even Mary, or so she admitted in a letter she wrote that night:

> Here we are, Everina; but my trembling hand will scarce let me tell you so. Bess is much more composed than I expected her to be; but to make my trial [her trial!] still more dreadful, I was afraid in the coach she was going to have one of her flights, for she bit her wedding-ring to pieces. When I can recollect myself, I'll send you particulars; but, at present, my heart beats time with every carriage that rolls by, and a knocking at the door almost throws me into a fit. I hope B. will not discover us, for I could sooner face a lion; yet the door never opens, but I expect to see him panting for breath. Ask Ned how we are to behave if he should find us out, for Bess is determined not to return. Can he force her? —but I'll not suppose it, yet I can think of nothing else. She is sleepy, and going to bed; my agitated mind will not permit me. Don't tell Charles [their youngest brother] or any creature. Oh! let me entreat you to be careful, for Bess does not dread him now so much as I do.[8]

And in a postscript to that letter Mary added a line that is surely one of the most remarkable of her record: "I almost wish for an husband, for I want somebody to support me."[9]

Well she might have wanted a supporter: what an outrageously highhanded thing to have done! The escape was carried through, one surmises, with a bull-like force that simply rolled Eliza along. Did she want to leave Mr. B. and her baby, did she bite her wedding ring from terror, despair, or indecision? No matter: "Bess is tolerably well," Mary wrote a few days later, when she had recovered her nerve and poise; "she cannot help sighing about little Mary, whom she tenderly loved; and on this score I both love and pity her. The poor brat! it had got a hold on my affections; some time or other I hope we shall get it. . . ."[10]

[7] *Ibid.*, p. 169.      [8] *Ibid.*      [9] *Ibid.*      [10] *Ibid.*, p. 170.

All in all, Mary thought, though it had been a "very disagreeable affair," though Eliza's mind was "harassed with the fear of being discovered and the thought of leaving the child," the escape had accomplished its purpose of delivering her from "extreme wretchedness." "Tell my brother that Bess is fixed in her resolution of never returning," Mary wrote to Everina, and "if a separate maintenance is not to be obtained, she'll try to earn her own bread."[11] She knew that she, Mary, would be judged the "shameful incendiary, in this shocking affair of a woman's leaving her bed-fellow," this action so "contrary to all the rules of conduct that are published for the benefit of new married ladies." But, she concluded, such "disorders will give way to time, if it brings a little tranquillity with it," and the "thought of having assisted to bring about so desirable an event, will ever give me pleasure to think of."[12]

The final word on this little drama is the development of Mary's ego within it. The whole thing is a powerful insight into her estrangement, her alienation, from normal social convention. Not that she was unaware of that convention: for a moment she was sufficiently dismayed by it to long for a "supporter," and to reflect that she would be blamed as a "shameful incendiary" by the arbiters of the "rules of conduct" (as she was, by offended matron-acquaintances who cut her thereafter).[13] But that moment was the deviation; one sees for the first time how completely Mary relied on her own perceptions and determinations. She still found, of course, comfort and self-justification in her religion. Onto the final letter to Everina about the affair she tacked this paragraph:

Don't suppose I am preaching, when I say uniformity of conduct cannot in any degree be expected from those whose first motive of action is not the pleasing the Supreme Being, and those who humbly rely on Providence will not only be supported in affliction, but have a Peace imparted to them that is past all describing. This state is indeed a warfare, and we learn little that we don't smart for in the attaining. The cant of weak enthusiasts

11 *Ibid.*    12 *Ibid.*, pp. 171, 170.    13 *Ibid.*, p. 171.

has made the consolations of Religion and the assistance of the Holy Spirit appear ridiculous to the inconsiderate, but it is the only solid foundation of comfort that the weak efforts of reason will be assisted and our hearts and minds corrected and improved till the time arrives when we shall not only see *perfection*, but see every creature around us happy. . . .[14]

The prose is appalling but its message is clear: why should she care about the disapproval of society when she had the Supreme Being on her side? Exactly how, by what steps, she had arrived at this self-sufficiency and self-righteousness is not so clear; but surely an answer lay in some triumphant sense she had about the life-style she was constructing, in her feeling that she had so consciously controlled her selfish, volatile self that she was automatically in a state of grace.

In comparison with her achievement in saving Eliza from the torments of a bad marriage, the problem of earning their bread —which Mary naturally assumed as her responsibility—seemed one that would dissolve at a touch. Mary had the bright idea, in the days immediately after the escape, that not only she and Eliza but dear Fanny as well could find lodgings and live together comfortably by needlework and Fanny's sketches. Her imagination racing with the plan, she wrote to Everina: "With economy we can live on a guinea a week, and that we can with ease earn. The lady who gave Fanny five guineas for two drawings will assist us and we shall be independent. . . . If Ned makes us a little present of furniture it will be very acceptable, but if he is prudent, we must try to do without it."[15] Eliza was no resistance to the force that Mary had become, but Fanny still had problems (or one problem: Hugh Skeys) and some will of her own. She wrote to Everina that she was "tortured" by Mary's and Eliza's plight, that she could see no "possible resource" for them, that she was frightened that Edward might be "displeased" about any connection of Mary with herself (why?), that with her drawings she could

[14] *Ibid.*     [15] *Ibid.*

earn no more than the manifestly insufficient sum of half a guinea a week, and that Mary's and Eliza's needlework would bring no more than "half-a-guinea between them, supposing they had constant employment, which is of all things the most uncertain." She suggested that the two girls forget about living with her, and forget as well Mary's impractical schemes of independence. The only possible thing for them to do, she thought, was to rely on the male, brother Edward, who might stock them into a small haberdashery shop. Then, still worried about Edward's disapproval, she added: "I wish you would take the earliest opportunity of assuring him from me *that on no* account whatever will I ever live with them unless fortune should make me quite independent, which I never expect."[16] Fanny, faithful to female reality-principle, had apparently blocked the project.

The contrast between Mary and her beloved timid friend was never more clear. In the words of *Mary:* "she loved Ann better than any one in the world," and "to snatch her from the very jaws of destruction—she would have encountered a lion. To have this friend constantly with her; to make her mind easy with respect to her family, would it not be superlative bliss?" Thus Mary so intended "to have a home to receive" Fanny in that "it drove every other desire out of her mind."[17] Evidently she was not inclined to ask brother Edward for a loan or gift toward a haberdashery or any other kind of shop, though she did need and somehow got money[18] to realize her own perhaps more ambitious plan.

For in 1784 Mary opened a day school in the north of London, first at Islington—briefly, and without promise—then in "one of the intellectual centers of the Dissenting interest," Newington Green.[19] There Mary won her point in making a "home" for Fanny, and for Eliza and Everina as well, in a house—gotten for an "enormous rent"—large enough for them and their teaching enterprise. The move was a heady success:

[16] *Ibid.*, pp. 171–172.    [17] Wollstonecraft, *Mary*, pp. 35–36.
[18] See Cameron, ed., *Shelley and His Circle*, I, 45.    [19] *Ibid.*, p. 55.

through the "exertions" of one of Mary's new friends, Mrs. James Burgh, widow of the author of *Political Disquisitions*, a book on the franchise that had become a "reformer's handbook,"[20] the school "in two or three weeks obtained near twenty scholars."[21] And Newington Green was an instructive, challenging place to live; Mary's "first" friend there was Dr. Richard Price, the moral philosopher of civil liberty whose home was a haven for distinguished liberals.[22] But most immediately important was that the girls were together, not in some lower-middle-class dead end of a retail shop, nor in hopeless positions of respectable female drudgery, but in a demanding and responsible occupation that carried independence and even prestige. (Mary's friends at the Green introduced her to Dr. Johnson, who treated her with "particular kindness and attention" and invited her to return often.)[23] Mary, age twenty-five, had done it all—again, with a bull-like force and an optimism that had simply brushed away the difficulties attending such female initiative.

But she hadn't yet enough to appease her managerial drive. Before the end of the year 1784 she had assumed as emotional and financial burdens her younger brothers James and Charles, whose career plans needed her direction, Fanny's younger brother George, who was involved in various scrapes, and the almost destitute Blood parents. Mary's own father would be in line for a kind of assistance in the next year or so, when his financial affairs had gotten so tangled that Mary would take them over and handle them "to the day of her death."[24] Nor was she done with Fanny, who was growing more seriously consumptive throughout the year at Newington Green, and still yearning for the elusive Hugh Skeys, by this time a merchant in Lisbon. Somehow an apparent solution for Fanny materialized. (Was Mary behind it? One would not put it past her, and her most careful biographer suspects her instiga-

[20] *Ibid.*, p. 56.
[21] *Ibid.*, p. 45 (letter from Everina Wollstonecraft to Godwin, 1797).
[22] Godwin, *Memoirs*, p. 29.     [23] *Ibid.*     [24] *Ibid.*, p. 48.

tion.)[25] From Lisbon Skeys finally proposed; and Mary, thinking of the medical opinion that Fanny must go to a southern climate, urged her to accept, even though she privately felt that Skeys was a vulgar mate for sensitive Fanny.[26]

Living for and through others, knowing their dependence on her initiative, drive, and courage—this is the life Mary had cut out for herself. She would remain fixed in it for a long time, till at least 1787, eight years of an attempt to win the posthumous approval of her mother, to approximate her girlhood image of the useful and the selfless. Objectively speaking, it could not have been a relaxed and pleasant life. "Mary had a quickness of temper," Godwin wrote, "not apt to take offence with inadvertencies, but which led her to look into the minds of her acquaintances, and to approve or to be displeased, in proportion as they manifested those sentiments, which the persons and the treatment they met with, ought, as she conceived, to excite. She was occasionally severe and imperious in her resentments; and, when she strongly disapproved, was apt to express her censure in terms that gave a very humiliating sensation to the person against whom it was directed."[27] An imperious, judgmental, censurious Mary must have been hard to deal with in day-to-day routines, especially for her sisters; Eliza, as we shall see, rarely passed up an opportunity in later years to express (though not to Mary) her spiteful resentment. Truly if Mary had set out in her role of benefactress in order to gain love and approval, the contradictions of her own nature denied her that goal.

But Mary didn't look at it from Eliza's or anyone else's point of view; what she was aware of was that it had not worked at all well for herself. It may be that Godwin squirmed a bit as he worked over this period of her life, as he conscientiously transmitted her sense of having been blameless in her dealings with a host of ingrates. For these years, he wrote, Mary

[25] Wardle, *Wollstonecraft*, p. 38.
[26] Paul, *Godwin*, I, 176 (letter to George Blood).
[27] Godwin, *Memoirs*, p. 33.

may be said to have been, in a great degree, the victim of a desire to promote the benefit of others. She did not foresee the severe disappointment with which an exclusive purpose of this sort is pregnant; she was inexperienced enough to lay a stress upon the consequent gratitude of those she benefited; and she did not sufficiently consider that, in proportion as we involve ourselves in the interests and society of others, we acquire a more exquisite sense of their defects, and are tormented with their untractableness and folly.[28]

Immediately following the precisely chosen words of that passage, Godwin added a parenthetical editorial comment that could only be a gentle judgment of the strong-willed lady who was his wife: "In the mixed scene of human life, it is necessary that, while we take some care for others, we should leave scope for the display of their own prudence and reason; and that, when we have discharged our duty respecting them, we should be habituated to derive a principal consolation from the consciousness of having done so."[29] So far was Mary from having her "principal consolation" in knowing she was helping others that the idea did not even occur to her in discussing her life with Godwin. It seems quite clear: what she had launched into after her mother's death was a frantic effort to find ego gratification, to appease her own powerful drive for creative independence, in managing, manipulating, possessing, the lives of those of her family and friends who were willing to allow her to do such things. And what she discovered was that the whole effort made her very unhappy.

In the summer of 1785 Mary wrote a letter to George Blood —who had become a special confidant—which contained these lines: "I have been very ill, and gone through the usual physical operations, have been bled and blistered, yet still am not well; my harassed mind will in time wear out my body. I have been so hunted down by cares, and see so many that I must encounter, that my spirits are quite depressed. I have lost all

[28] *Ibid.*, pp. 35–36.    [29] *Ibid.*, p. 36.

relish for life, and my almost broken heart is only cheered by the prospect of death. I may be years a-dying tho', and so I ought to be patient, for at this time to wish myself away would be selfish."[30] Shades of Elizabeth Wollstonecraft!—what had happened to cause such verbal despair? Perhaps it was just the end of a long, trying day and Mary's patience with pupils and boarders and sisters had snapped; perhaps, late at night, she was simply indulging in a bit of self-dramatization and self-pity. But the tone and complaints continue in a following letter: "Labour and sorrow fill up my time, and so I toil through this vale of tears—and all this leads to an end which will be happy if I faint not." And she shared with George, who was apparently a high-spirited, happy-go-lucky young man, her own "gloomy kind of resignation": "Be not cast down while we are struggling with care, life slips away, and, through the assistance of Divine Grace, we are obtaining habits of virtue that will enable us to relish those joys that we cannot now form any idea of."[31]

When she told George Blood, "I amost hate the Green, for it seems the grave of all my comforts,"[32] Mary had some reason for loneliness and depression. Fanny's departure had left a gaping hole in her life (though she was delighted to hear of Fanny's happiness and improving health in Lisbon), and then George, too, had "gone over the hills and far away." Her sisters she considered impossible companions: "I have no creature to be unreserved to," she complained; "Eliza and Everina are so different that I could as soon fly as open my heart to them."[33] There is also the story that she had had her first unhappy love attachment at the Green, that perhaps she had just been jilted, in that summer of 1785, by a worldly, sophisticated young clergyman named Joshua Waterhouse.[34] If this were true—and the evidence is not conclusive—it would fit, would contribute to an explanation of her laments about all her

[30] Paul, *Godwin*, I, 174.    [31] *Ibid.*, pp. 174–175.    [32] *Ibid.*
[33] *Ibid.*
[34] See Elizabeth Nitchie, "An Early Suitor of Mary Wollstonecraft," *PMLA*, LVIII (1943), 164–169. Also Wardle, *Wollstonecraft*, pp. 41–43.

"social comforts" dropping away. Perhaps these were the things behind her morose letters to George Blood.

But the probability is that there was a deeper source of Mary's depression, and that was the psychological incongruity of the mother-identity she was trying to live. She had arranged her life in a most peculiar way: she was actor, initiator, director, controller, of other peoples' lives and destinies. Theoretically, her own was to be shaped and filled in the very act of that selfless devotion. Instead what she was left with was a quite selfish sense of unfulfillment, of emptiness and pointlessness, of the absolute dead end that was her own existence. So she had achieved financial independence, made a home for her sisters, was increasingly responsible for her brothers and father and the Bloods—so it was all dull, tasteless, almost without satisfaction and wholly without joy. And perhaps her neighbors and acquaintances at Newington Green—Dr. Price, his frequent visitor Joseph Priestley, the Reverend John Hewlett, who would later be of special assistance to her—intensified her unhappiness and discontent. Perhaps the example of these knowledgeable and talented people, involved in and dedicated to politics and science and literature, simply made more unbearable the vacuum of her own life's achievements. Coming out of such a well of dissatisfaction, Mary's letters to George Blood would be but two faint cries of despair.

Toward the end of 1785 Mary's self-created world began to crumble, the causes external and very, very real. Fanny in Portugal was to have a baby, and nothing could dissuade Mary from going to Lisbon to be nurse and companion during the confinement. Leaving her school in her sisters' care and borrowing money for her passage, Mary sailed to Fanny's side; she arrived in Lisbon just hours before the birth of Fanny's son and was in constant vigil until, a few days later, both mother and baby died. Back in England after a ghastly sea voyage, she found that Eliza and Everina had been inadequate substitutes in the school, that her pupils were dropping away, and her boarders leaving in indignation. Within two months, with Mary deep in debt, the school had to be abandoned; sisters Everina and Eliza were prepared to "go out into the world," hopefully "the one as a companion, and the other as a teacher," and Mary planned to live on alone at the Green, taking "cheap lodging" and a few "scholars."[35]

This was terrible trouble, the most searing sorrow and bitter defeat of Mary's life. She wrote George Blood,

I have lost all relish for pleasure, and life seems a burden too heavy to be endured. My head is stupid, and my heart sick and exhausted. . . . The loss of Fanny was sufficient of itself to have thrown a cloud over my brightest days: what effect then must it have, when I am bereft of every other comfort? I have too many debts. I cannot think of remaining any longer in this house, the rent is so enormous, and where to go, without money or friends, who can point out? My eyes are very bad and my memory gone. I am not fit for any situation, and as for Eliza, I don't know what will become of her. My constitution is impaired, I hope I shan't live long, yet I may be a tedious time dying.[36]

From Ireland, George Blood suggested that she leave England and settle near him. She answered:

. . . my future prospects are still more gloomy—yet nothing should induce me to fly from England. My creditors have a right to do what they please with me, should I not be able to satisfy their demands. I am almost afraid to look forward, tho' I am convinced that the same Providence that brought me through past difficulties, will still continue to protect me. Should our present plan fail, I cannot even guess what the girls will do. My brother, I am sure, will not receive them, and they are not calculated to struggle with the world. Eliza, in particular, is very helpless. Their situation has made me very uneasy,—and as to your father and mother, they have been a continual weight on my spirits. You have removed part of the load, for I now hope you would be able to keep them from perishing, should my affairs grow desperate,— and this hope has made me very grateful—for often when I have thought of death as the only end of my sorrows and cares, I earnestly wished to see them settled before I went to *rest*.[37]

[35] Paul, *Godwin*, I, 183.        [36] *Ibid.*, pp. 179–180.
[37] Wardle, *Wollstonecraft*, p. 47.

Three months later Mary had apparently lost the will to act:

> I have done with all worldly pursuits and wishes; I only desire
> to submit without being dependent on the caprice of our fellow
> creatures. I shall have many solitary hours, but I have not much to
> hope for in life, and so it would be absurd to give way to fear. I
> am trying to do my duty in that station in which Providence has
> placed me, I shall enjoy some tranquil moments, and the pleasures
> I have the greatest relish for are not entirely out of my reach . . .
> I have been trying to muster up my fortitude, and labouring for
> patience to bear my many trials. . . .[38]

No one would doubt Mary's anguish at losing Fanny or her
disappointment at the collapse of her school. But it is possible
to be skeptical about the reality of her rhetoric of pious
resignation, which by this time was overworked; the truth is
that the very desperation of her situation moved her to energetic activity. While she was dissolving the school she wrote a
book, dashed it off, actually, probably at the urging of John
Hewlett, who took it to Joseph Johnson, the London book-
seller, and got not only a promise of publication but ten
guineas.[39] With that money Mary sent Mr. and Mrs. Blood to
Ireland for a new start (and to be near George), paid some of
her own debts, and resettled her sisters. She was positively
relieved with the last accomplishment. She had developed,
Godwin wrote, "a rooted aversion to that sort of cohabitation
with her sisters, which the project of the school imposed.
Cohabitation is a point of delicate experiment, and is, in the
majority of instances, pregnant with ill-humour and unhappiness." Her "kindness" to Eliza and Everina, he added, "was not
diminished, but she resolved that the mode of its exertion in
future should be different, tending to their benefit, without
intrenching upon her own liberty."[40]

"Her own liberty"—this was the goal that was revitalizing
Mary, even as she moaned to George Blood that "the prison
walls are decaying, and the prisoner will ere long get

[38] Paul, *Godwin*, I, 183.      [39] Godwin, *Memoirs*, p. 37.
[40] *Ibid.*, p. 38.

free. . . ."[41] How thoroughly she had concealed herself from herself in her overlong adolescence. She *had* won "liberty" and an amazing stretch of independence, given the realities for an obscure young woman in the England of the 1780's. Yet now it was a "prison," this morass of female responsibilities she had arranged for herself. It took eight years and a few hard blows to make her see that her happiness did not consist of encouraging dependents to hang onto her petticoats. But she was ready now to look for something beyond the dubious rewards of Universal Benevolence and a "matriarchate," to search out other, better ways to win love, esteem, and the power and self-confidence of independent independence.

[41] Paul, *Godwin*, I, 183.

# Chapter Five

# THE APPRENTICE AUTHOR

. . . Your sex generally laugh at female determinations; but let me tell you, I never yet resolved to do, any thing of consequence, that I did not adhere resolutely to it, till I had accomplished my purpose. . . .

Letter to Joseph Johnson

. . . Woman is still astonished and flattered at being admitted to the world of thought, of art—a masculine world. She is on her best behavior. . . .

*The Second Sex*

*L*ET there be no underestimation of the effect of Newington Green on Mary's ambitions. Without that experience among accomplished radical people she likely would have remained a dissatisfied school-marm, with no more vision than to impart the lessons of self-discipline to the young. Mary was a natural for radical liberalism, naturally drawn to circles whose ideology did not include an immediate rejection of women as women, as insignificant beings whose achievements were automatically inferior to those of men. And most essential to her confidence, she learned from people like Richard Price the absolute morality of rationally directed individual freedom of expression, the virtue and value of the independent and fearless quest for one's own truth.

But it was her own dogged will that carried Mary into an independent writing career; she had no patron or benefactor (Hewlett was neither), nor did she fall by accident into authorship. Rather, she resolved to write a book, she chose to be an author—a decision aimed, of course, at solving her financial problems but nevertheless extraordinarily bold. There had been no one in her family with intellectual inclinations, no one to provide her with any sort of literary precedent except her new friends at the Green. This rerouting, at a time when she was deep in despair, when, one would think, her mental energies were at an absolute ebb, was one of the remarkable moments of the remarkable process that was Mary's life.

The effort that earned her ten guineas from the publisher Joseph Johnson was a didactic, moralizing little book built entirely out of her experience (necessarily, for what else did she know?). Entitled in full, *Thoughts on the Education of Daughters; with Reflections on Female Conduct, in the more important Duties of Life*, it is filled helter-skelter with Mary-like attitudes and admonitions, all of them, as usual, "intensely self-revealing." For example: "The governing of our temper is truly the business of our whole lives," and success in it only comes when "reason gains some strength." Yet, dwelling on the "presence of the Deity" with "habitual reverence" is the chief way to handle anger, for "exalted views will raise the mind above trifling cares, and the many little weaknesses, which make us a torment to ourselves and others." And when a weak woman is dominated by her husband she "will as unreasonably tyrannifie over her servants," since "slavish fear and tyranny go together."[1] She devoted an interesting chapter to what she had learned, first-hand, about employment prospects of the young gentlewoman left without provision by her parents. Reviewing the three unappealing alternatives the girl has—being a governess or a companion, or with more skills, teaching—she observed that the "few trades which are left are now gradually falling into the hands of the men, and certainly they are not very respectable." What in the world could such an unfortunate young woman do to make her life interesting and effective? Nothing, really, but she "ought not to be discontented. Good must ultimately arise from everything, to those who look beyond this infancy of their being; and here

[1] Wollstonecraft, *Thoughts on the Education of Daughters*, pp. 61–67.

the comfort of a good conscience is our only stable support. The main business of our lives is to learn to be virtuous."[2] On the problems of love, she pointed out that "the heart is very treacherous, and if we do not guard its first emotions, we shall not afterwards be able to prevent its sighing for impossibilities"; in any case love is a distraction, for "universal benevolence is the first duty, and we should be careful not to let any passion, so engross our thoughts, as to prevent our practicing it."[3] To all of her topics Mary applied the same hard line: life is weary and difficult, made deliberately so by "the Almighty," the "kind parent, who chastens and educates, and indulges us not when it would tend to our hurt." Action, then, is useless and acceptance of God's will the only human way—with hope, hope that it all works out to a "far more exceeding and eternal weight of glory."[4]

But despite the language of resignation Mary was not resigned to an invisible fate; instead, here in 1786, she was busily working out the reorientation of her life. Late in the year she was offered the position of governess in the family of Lord Kingsborough in Ireland at the rate of forty pounds a year. "I by no means like the proposal of being a governess," she told George Blood,[5] but she took the job. Her idea was that in a year she would pay the rest of her debts,[6] settle Eliza somewhere (unlucky Everina went back to live with Edward), and still have enough to start herself in her new career. "Independence," wrote Godwin, "was the object after which she thirsted, and she was fixed to try whether it might not be found in literary occupation. She was desirous however first to accumulate a small sum of money, which should enable her to consider at leisure the different literary engagements that might offer, and provide in some degree for the eventual

[2] *Ibid.*, pp. 71–78.    [3] *Ibid.*, pp. 89–91.    [4] *Ibid.*, pp. 78, 109.
[5] Paul, *Godwin*, I, 184.
[6] See the discussion in Cameron, ed., *Shelley and His Circle*, I, 85–87, about Mary's problems in repaying money she borrowed from Mrs. James Burgh to settle her school debts in Newington Green and travel to Ireland.

deficiency of her earliest attempts."[7] In short, behind the fu-
nereal habit-screen of surrender to the blows of life was a
steady pulsing of purposeful activity.

Mary's letters from her Irish exile are a study in contradiction (and one sympathizes with her sisters if they were confused in reading them). The dominant tone is self-pitying
lament. Entering the great gates of Kingsborough Castle, she
told Everina, was like "going into the Bastille"; "I must labour
for content," she added, "and try to reconcile myself to a state
which is contrary to every feeling of my soul."[8] Inside the
castle it was even worse: there she was "confined to the society
of a set of silly females," who exhausted her with "their
boisterous spirits and unmeaning laughter" ("not forgetting
hourly domestic bickerings").[9] "I am very ill," she continued to
Everina, "and so low-spirited my tears flow in torrents almost
insensibly [!]. I struggle with myself, but I hope my Heavenly
Father will not be extreme to mark my weakness, and that He
will have compassion of a poor bruised reed, and pity a miserable wretch, whose sorrows He only knows."[10] On the other
hand, Mary had energy in this orgy of introspection to dissect
coolly the manners of the aristocratic ladies of her new environment. She acidly described (in the very same letter to
Everina) the "dissipated lives led by the women of quality,"
and observed that "in many respects the great and little vulgar
resemble each other, and in none more than in the motives
which induce them to marry." Lady Kingsborough, who
would be the model for idle, indolent, and self-centered rich
females in Mary's fiction, was handled with fine bourgeois
scorn: "Lady K's passion for animals fills up the hours which
are not spent in dressing. . . . I think now I hear her infantine
lisp. She rouges—and in short is a fine lady, without fancy or
sensibility."[11] Apparently from the beginning she was accepted
in the convivial life of the castle, and was quite pleased with
her social self: "I make allowance and adapt myself, talk of
getting husbands for the *Ladies*—and the *dogs*, and am won-

[7] Godwin, *Memoirs*, p. 39.    [8] Paul, *Godwin*, I, 185.
[9] *Ibid.*, p. 187.    [10] *Ibid.*, p. 188.    [11] *Ibid.*, p. 187.

derfully entertaining."[12] Perhaps Everina wondered when her sister had time to let her "tears flow in torrents."

Much as she complained about it, the year as a governess for the Irish aristocracy was a good one for Mary. She was coming out of her overlong adolescence, out of her attempt to emulate a fantasy figure of mother-identity, out of her futile efforts to live through others. Necessarily it was a very self-involved year, with much self-indulgence, the reports of which are indeed, in ways Mary couldn't know, "wonderfully entertaining." Her relationship with Lady Kingsborough must have been based on mutual detestation. Soon after she arrived she wrote Eliza that "Lady K. is very civil, nay kind, yet I cannot help fearing her."[13] It is impossible to imagine Mary being obsequious, especially in a situation in which she felt at a disadvantage; she would be more apt to irritate than ingratiate. She rapidly took over the Kingsborough children—their affection as well as their education—with a more than dutiful intervention that was essential, she explained in letters to her sisters, because of the mother's selfishness and disinterest.[14] *That* judgment must have been implied in her contacts with Lady Kingsborough (and in fact it would be on such an issue that she would be dismissed from the Kingsborough service). One gets an image of a year of constant, polite warfare between the two women.

And Mary was unconsciously most funny in the letters that told of the gay round of balls and parties to which she was taken by the Kingsboroughs and their friends. This was a new situation, one demanding a new personality; sure enough, in a few months Mary had acquired what she clearly thought an interesting social manner. She was the secretly sorrowing heroine of popular fiction, a sufferer who bravely bore troubles so deep that they inflicted her with mysterious maladies—and gratifying it must have been that her malaise was given diagnostic status by Lady Kingsborough's personal physician as "constant nervous fever." As she told Everina,

12 *Ibid.*, p. 188.    13 Godwin, *Memoirs,* Supplement, p. 167.
14 *Ibid.*, p. 40.

Indeed it is impossible to enumerate the various complaints I am troubled with, and how much my mind is harassed by them. I know they all arise from disordered nerves, that are injured beyond a *possibility* of receiving *any* aid from medicine. There is no cure for a broken heart! It is true, it may languidly perform its *animal* functions—but it can no longer be *inflated* with hope. The nervous fever I am subject to has increased my natural sensibility to such a degree I may with reason complain of the irritability of my nerves. I want a tender nurse—I want—but it matters not. . . .[15]

Carried away with her vision of her sensitive, suffering, tragic self, she explained to Everina (whose reaction one wishes one knew) that

deprived of the only comforts I can relish, I give way to whim. And yet when the most sprightly sallies burst from me, the tear frequently trembles in my eye, and the long drawn sigh eases my full heart—so my eyes roll in the wild way you have *seen* them. A deadly paleness overspreads my countenance—and yet so weak am I a sudden thought or any recollected emotion of tenderness will occasion the most painful suffusion. You know not, my dear Girl, of what materials this strange inconsistent heart of mine is formed, and how alive it is to tenderness and misery. Since I have been here I have turned over several pages in the vast volume of human nature, and what is the amount? Vanity and vexation of spirit—and yet I am *tied* to my fellow-creatures by partaking of their weaknesses. I rail at a fault—sicken at the sight—and find it stirring within me. New sympathies and feelings *start* up. I know not myself.—"Tis these whims," Mr. Ogle tells me, "render me interesting"—and Mrs. Ogle with a placid smile quotes some of my own sentiments—while I cry the physician *cannot* heal himself.[16]

All of this is very, very good: Mary the self-creating, open to models, here taking bits and pieces of the influences of her environment into the uncompleted entity that was her ego, constructing a grotesque kind of image the inadequacy of which she was yet aware—"I know not myself." It was also

[15] Wardle, *Wollstonecraft*, pp. 68–69.     [16] *Ibid.*, p. 69.

very feminine, girlish even, as though she were reliving at
Kingsborough Castle an adolescence that had surely had an
insufficiency of teen-age pleasure (silliness?). The Mr. Ogle,
the friend of the Kingsboroughs she mentioned, was George
Ogle, an authentic romantic figure—an Irish poet who was
born and bred to sing of a lovely land of rugged cliffs and
broad green valleys. But he was also a hard-headed politician
and statesman, MP for the county of Wexford, an Irish whig
and proper associate of an enlightened landlord-capitalist like
Lord Kingsborough. This side of Mr. Ogle—or Lord Kingsborough—Mary mentioned not at all (a decided contrast to
the Mary of ten years later, who would pride herself on being
a "woman of observation," who in her international travels
asked "men's questions").[17] A female, a romantic, a sentimen-
talist—Mary was playing with roles, trying them on, and
enjoying herself hugely. She was reading *Emile*, she told her
sister, and "loving" Rousseau's "paradoxes." Rousseau, she explained, "rambles into that chimerical world in which I have
too often wandered, and draws the usual conclusion that all is
vanity and vexation of spirit. He was a strange, inconsistent,
unhappy, clever creature, yet he possessed an uncommon portion of sensibility and penetration."[18] "Sensibility" was the
quality that fascinated her; she would define it in one of her
early works as

the result of acute senses, finely fashioned nerves, which vibrate
at the slightest touch, and convey such clear intelligence to the
brain, that it does not require to be arranged by the judgment.
Such persons instantly enter into the character of others, and
instinctively discern what will give pain to every human being;
their own feelings are so varied that they seem to contain in
themselves, not only all the passions of the species, but their
various modifications. Exquisite pain and pleasure is their portion; nature wears for them a different aspect than is displayed to
common mortals. One moment it is a paradise; all is beautiful: a

[17] Wollstonecraft, *Letters from Sweden*, p. 13.
[18] Paul, *Godwin*, I, 189.

cloud arises, an emotion receives a sudden damp; darkness invades the sky, and the world is an unweeded garden.[19]

And she herself was writing her first novel, in whose (semi-) fictional "Mary" she was trying to illustrate the sensibility and exquisite emotionality of an uncommon mortal.

The nature of these experiments may seem funny, but their intention by the end of the Kingsborough year was in dead earnest. Mary talked of her new self for the first time in a letter to sister Eliza in June of 1787, reporting that she was reading "Philosophy" and writing, then adding—with pardonable self-importance—"I *hope* you have not forgotten that I am an Author."[20] In the next month she came to London with the Kingsboroughs, where they were all to stop briefly before going on to a summer tour of the Continent; it was here that Mary was dismissed by Lady Kingsborough, the "pretext" being the childrens' distress at her leaving for a few days to visit her family.[21] It was perfect timing: in August Mary took her manuscript of *Mary* to Joseph Johnson; he agreed to publish it and promised her besides steady writing work and even lodgings at his own house until she got settled in the city. Mary the author, the independent woman, was on her way.

There are two letters that are particularly valuable keys to Mary's mind and emotions in this interim period, this moment before her entry into the world of the professional writer. The first is a letter telling Everina of her new situation, a note in which the old and the new, the hurt and the proud, the insecure and the overweening, the dutiful and the egoistic, the dependent and the independent—all these Marys are expressed:

Mr. Johnson, whose uncommon kindness, I believe, has saved me from despair and vexation, I shrink back from, and feared to encounter, assures me that if I exert my talents in writing I may support myself in a comfortable way. I am then going to be the

[19] Godwin, *Posthumous Works, Cave of Fancy,* IV, 135–136.
[20] Wardle, *Wollstonecraft,* p. 72.
[21] Godwin, *Memoirs,* Supplement, p. 170.

first of a new genus; I tremble at the attempt, yet if I fail *I* only suffer, and should I succeed my dear girls will ever in sickness have a home, and a refuge, where for a few months in the year they may forget the cares that disturb the rest. . . . I would not on any account inform my father or Edward of my designs—you and Eliza are the only part of the family I am interested about, I wish to be a mother to you both. My undertaking would subject me to ridicule, and an inundation of friendly advice to which I cannot listen; I must be independent. . . . This project has long floated in my mind. You know I am not born to tread in the beaten track, the peculiar bent of my nature pushes me on.[22]

The second is to Joseph Johnson, written after she had left his house but before she had found rooms in London. One guesses she was uncertain about hitting the right note with Johnson. She opens with a pretentious bit about wandering by the Thames, listening to the song of a robin and the noise of a water mill with only "partial attention," for she was at the same time "discussing some knotty point, or straying from this *tiny* world to new systems." Johnson might have smiled at such intellectual airs, but surely he found irresistible the Mary who emerged in the next lines:

I was just going to mend my pen; but I believe it will enable me to say all I have to add to this epistle. Have you yet heard of an habitation for me? I often think of my new plan of life; and, list my sister [she was visiting Eliza] should try to prevail on me to alter it, I have avoided mentioning it to her. I am determined! —Your sex generally laugh at female determinations; but let me tell you, I never yet resolved to do, any thing of consequence, that I did not adhere resolutely to it, till I had accomplished my purpose, improbable as it might have appeared to a more timid mind. In the course of near nine-and-twenty years, I have gathered some experience, and felt many severe disappointments—and what is the amount? I long for a little peace and *independence!* Every obligation we receive from our fellow-creatures is a new shackle, takes from our native freedom, and debases the mind, makes us mere earthworms—I am not fond of grovelling![23]

[22] Paul, *Godwin*, I, 191–192.
[23] Godwin, *Posthumous Works, Letters to Johnson*, IV, 64–65.

That paragraph was Mary's manifesto, the summing of the past and a declaration of her future.

And 1787–1788 was a great divide in Mary's life. Through Johnson she published *Mary* and a children's book entitled *Original Stories from Real Life; with Conversations, Calculated to Regulate the Affections, and Form the Mind to Truth and Goodness.* The two were quite different works, the first referring back to the Mary of introspection and self-pity, the second (which sold well, and went into a second edition with engravings by William Blake as its chief distinction) a rigorous exercise in the liberal faith she was acquiring, a formidably pedantic tract intended indeed to form the youthful mind to rational direction of its every activity. In 1788 Johnson and his friend Thomas Christie started a magazine, the *Analytical Review,* and with its first issue in May, Mary had a regular job, and a steady income, as a reviewer and translator.

Joseph Johnson opened a brilliant world to Mary, in his invitation to join the circle of friends who gathered for talk in his shop, or for his "famous weekly dinners"[24] in the rooms above at No. 72 St. Paul's Churchyard. The list of Johnson's visiting friends and authors reads like a catalog of late eighteenth-century English radical intellectualism: Price, Priestley, and Hewlett came there, of course. Others were scientific buffs like the mathematician John Bonnycastle, the eminent physician Dr. George Fordyce, "romantic" painter Henry Fuseli, Sarah Trimmer, whose *History of the Robins* Mary must have had in mind when she wrote her *Original Stories,* Anna Barbauld, William Blake, Tom Paine, Horne Tooke. And there came people close to Mary later—the Thomas Christies, the Joel Barlows, Mary Hays, Godwin himself.[25] This became Mary's circle and these her friends; among them, as Godwin wrote, she "was insensibly advancing towards a vigorous maturity. . . . The society she frequented, nourished her understanding, and enlarged her mind . . . gave a freedom and firmness to the expression of her sentiments."[26]

[24] Cameron, ed., *Shelley and His Circle,* I, 69.
[25] *Ibid.;* Godwin, *Memoirs,* p. 49.    [26] Godwin, *Memoirs,* p. 50.

And Mary's relations with her family were taking a significant new turn. She was still very much responsible for its welfare, probably more so than before, but the neurotic involvement was gone, replaced by a new brisk maturity. Everina she packed off to Paris, to improve her French and thus become a more marketable teacher. Eliza was placed in a school in Putney, near London, first as a "parlour boarder, and afterwards as a teacher." Her younger brothers were handled with dispatch too. James was "sent to Woolwich for instruction, to qualify him for a respectable situation in the royal navy, where he was shortly after made a lieutenant." Charles lived with her in London for a time, was articled, unsuccessfully, to an attorney, then sent to a farmer for an apprenticeship Mary hoped would fit him for emigration to America.[27] The caretaking of her brothers and sisters (and her father as well) was a heavy drain on Mary's income—according to Johnson, she spent no less than 200 pounds on her family in this period[28]—but at least she was putting them at a distance.

It was an exhilarating plunge that Mary had taken; it seems, too, a straightforward, self-reliant development, based sturdily on her undivided resolution for personal achievement. And that it was, except—"I know not myself," she had written at Kingsborough Castle: here as a London journalist she was again baffled, this time by what were to her inexplicable periods of painful depression. The reasons are probably not mysterious. Mary had been ten years on her own, but what her initiative had led to now was not within the safe categories of "women's work," was on the contrary "real" and challenging in a way that made her experience, her "warfare" for independence, seem almost inconsequential. She was reading, studying, learning languages—and realizing her deficiencies of education and training in comparison with the talented people she met, knowing plainly her handicaps and limitations in the man's business she had entered. She was trying to understand and to live the liberal rationality of the fascinating artists and

[27] Godwin, *Memoirs*, pp. 47–48.
[28] Johnson MSS in Paul, *Godwin*, I, 194.

writers of Johnson's circle, measuring herself against self-confident professionals, and under the kind of pressure to accept uncritically their ideas, their philosophy, that went against the grain of her own strong mind and dominating personality. She was alone in a demanding, judgmental world, and feeling more than ever before the loneliness that had been a constant in her life—in the little girl hurt by her mother's disinterest in her thoughts, in the adolescent who turned to God in her alienation from her family, in the young woman who "could as soon fly" as confide in her sisters. On the edge of ambitious, male-like, independence and responsibility, Mary was woman enough for moments of desperate insecurity and doubt; and in those moments she desperately needed sympathy and support.

Perhaps there were others, but it was Joseph Johnson who did service in Mary's depressions in these months. Whatever the condition and atmosphere of the lodging she had taken for herself in George Street in London, she spent a good deal of her time out and "most of her evenings" with Johnson.[29] She needed, apparently, simply to talk, and Johnson was somehow capable of listening. The record is sufficient to suggest something of them both—Mary voluble, self-involved, self-dramatizing, yet "incapable of disguise"; Johnson patient, tolerant, generous, but at times short with excesses of female self-pity. Mary's few notes to him mirrored her emotional tension as they continued the conversations: "You made me very low-spirited last night, by your manner of talking.—You are my only friend—the only person I am intimate with.—I never had a father, or a brother—you have been both to me, ever since I knew you—yet I have sometimes been very petulant.—I have been thinking of those instances of ill-humour and quickness, and they appear like crimes."[30] Or this: "I am trying to brace my nerves that I may be industrious.—I am afraid reason is not a good bracer—for I have been reasoning a long time with my

[29] Ibid.
[30] Godwin, Posthumous Works, Letters to Johnson, IV, 75.

untoward spirits—and yet my hand trembles."[31] And there is this long self-exploration, which recalls her love for Rousseau, though it is strikingly not affectation but a cry of some special anguish:

I am a mere animal, and instinctive emotions too often silence the suggestions of reason. Your note—I can scarcely tell why, hurt me—and produced a kind of winterly smile, which diffuses a beam of despondent tranquillity over the features. I have been very ill—Heaven knows it was more than fancy—After some sleepless, wearisome nights, towards the morning I have grown delirious. . . . My nerves were in such a painful state of irritation —I suffered more than I can express—Society was necessary—and might have diverted me till I gained more strength; but I blushed when I recollected how often I had teazed you with childish complaints, and the reveries of a disordered imagination. I even imagined that I intruded on you, because you never called on me —though you perceived that I was not well.—I have nourished a sickly kind of delicacy, which gives me many unnecessary pangs. —I acknowledge that life is but a jest—and often a frightful dream—yet catch myself every day searching for something seri-ous—and feel real misery from the disappointment. I am a strange compound of weakness and resolution! However, if I must suffer, I will endeavor to suffer in silence. There is certainly a great defect in my mind—my wayward heart creates its own misery— Why I am made thus I cannot tell; and, till I can form some idea of the whole of my existence, I must be content to weep and dance like a child—long for a toy, and be tired of it as soon as I get it.

We must each of us wear a fool's cap; but mine, alas! has lost its bells, and is grown so heavy, I find it intolerably troublesome. —Good-night! I have been pursuing a number of strange thoughts since I began to write, and have actually both wept and laughed immoderately—Surely I am a fool—[32]

What did Mary want from Johnson in this strange, troubled letter? Love, fatherly affection, total approval, male support for the weak female she was, his strength to quiet her "way-ward" heart, to correct the "great defect" in her mind—surely

[31] *Ibid.*, p. 89.      [32] *Ibid.*, pp. 76–78.

all these things. On the edge of her leap into freedom, she was a frightened, unloved child. Perhaps she was reaching too far. Perhaps she didn't really want independence and the terrible responsibility of her own life.

And yet, the heaviness of the fool's cap, the weakness and trembling of the midnight despair, could be wiped away by the cold light of Monday morning work. Mary told Johnson (actually on a Monday morning)

I really want a German grammar, as I intend to attempt to learn that language—and I will tell you the reason why.—While I live, I am persuaded, I must exert my understanding to procure an independence, and render myself useful. To make the task easier, I ought to store my mind with knowledge—the seed-time is passing away. I see the necessity of labouring now—and of that necessity I do not complain; on the contrary, I am thankful that I have more than common incentives to pursue knowledge, and draw my pleasures from the employments that are within my reach. You perceive this is not a gloomy day—I feel at this moment particularly grateful to you—without your humane and delicate assistance, how many obstacles should I not have had to encounter—too often should I have been out of patience with my fellow-creatures, whom I wish to love! Allow me to love you, my dear sir, and call friend a being I respect.[33]

It was a new day, a different mood, and another Mary—tough, determined, in charge of herself and her future.

[33] *Ibid.*, pp. 79–80.

*Chapter Six*

# THE INDEPENDENT WOMAN
### PART I

. . . and let me remind you that when weakness claims
indulgence, it seems to justify the despotism of
strength.

*Letter to Mary Hays*

. . . traditional woman is a . . . practitioner of bam-
boozlement; she attempts to disguise her dependence
from herself, which is a way of consenting to it. To
expose this dependence is in itself a liberation; a
clear-sighted cynicism is a defense against humilia-
tions and shame: it is the preliminary sketch of an
assumption.

*The Second Sex*

*M*ARY moved so fast from 1788 to 1792 that it is hard
to find in the woman of that period the self-consciously selfless patron of the weak from Newington Green, or the flighty young actress of Kingsborough
Castle, or even the uncertain, striving writer who had just
joined Johnson's staff. These were years of triumph, of light-
ning achievement that surpassed her most daring fancies, years
of gratification and prestige that soothed her insecurities and
swelled her ego (some might have thought to unseemly pro-
portions), years, too, in which she experimented, in a novel
kind of way, with love. She became, according to her own
fashion, the Independent Woman, living to the hilt an identity
which was more compatible to her nature than any she had
attempted before.

From the first issue of the *Analytical Review* in 1788, Mary
wrote furiously to earn her living at the various reviewing

tasks assigned to her by her employer, Joseph Johnson. At the beginning she was properly restricted to "female" topics, education, religion, morals, mostly through the medium of literature for middle-class ladies and children. The important matters that occupied the prime space in the liberal *Review*, science, technology, history, philosophy, politics, were beyond her knowledge, and perhaps she was content to let it go at that. The Mary of *Thoughts on the Education of Daughters* or the *Original Stories* is still recognizable in these early reviews, a lady dispensing homely, no-nonsense advice on the paths to virtue; she was reasonable, pedantic, moralizing, and bourgeois. A consistent critical standard runs through her reviews of novels of the day, most of them for and many by women: bad fiction was any literary work that encouraged feminine "sensuality," that stressed physical appearances or pleasures of the senses, that perpetuated, in short, thoughtlessness and eroticism in the female. And so her reviews were full of hard, adjectival rejection: one book, a "female production" and praiseworthy for its initial "modesty and delicacy," was marred by a passage dwelling on the "beauty" of the heroine's lover, an unnecessary description and moreover a "breach of decorum." A piece offered as "Evening Amusement for the Ladies" was dismissed as "trite," and a novel built around a situation in which both mother and daughter love the same man was "disgusting." Quoting a lady author who wrote, "so gentle, so forgiving, is the nature of a virtuous female; and so prone are we to love the offender, yet detest the offence," Mary observed tartly that "this is the varnish of sentiment to hide sensuality."[1]

"It perhaps deserves to be remarked," Godwin wrote, "that this sort of miscellaneous literary employment, seems, for the time at least, rather to damp and contract, than to enlarge and invigorate, the genius."[2] Godwin was not typically so obtuse. Not only was Mary sharpening her ideas about the capabilities of her sex (in the November, 1790, issue she did a lead review

[1] *Analytical Review*, II (1788), 223; III (1789), 221, 67–69, 222.
[2] Godwin, *Memoirs*, p. 46.

of Catherine Macaulay's *Letters on Education,* and judged it a work of "reason and profound thought," which "either through defective organs, or a mistaken education, seldom appears in female productions"),[3] and not only was she developing in self-confident exercise of her craft. She was learning furiously too, translating French and German works—in the January, 1789, *Review* she did a featured translation and review of Necker's *Importance of Religious Opinions*—and reading history and philosophy with a scholar's care. She was growing intellectually and catching up, even as she ground out her women's articles, with the revolutionary issues that were exploding about her.

There can be no doubt that her days were obsessively organized around her professional progress. Living alone in her George Street room, buried in study, meeting a heavy load of review assignments, she was much too absorbed to bother with her physical self and, beyond bare sustenance, her physical needs. She was frugal to the edge of asceticism; in the words of one (unfriendly) acquaintance, she "scarcely tasted animal food, or allowed herself the necessaries of life," and "her clothes were scarcely decent in her situation of life."[4] Such a standard of living reflected, of course, that price of Mary's independence which was support of her family; and one other explanation was that she lived abstemiously in ideological commitment to the "notions of privation which some of the revolutionists in France were now endeavouring to inculcate."[5] But self-denial carried, as Mary did it, to the point (in the common reproach) of "neglecting herself," of disdaining feminine "charms"—as her sisters described her attitude[6]—is a certain clue to the female intellectual. And thus one can imagine the professional Mary, bustling to St. Paul's Churchyard, probably with a thick bundle of manuscripts under her arm: a "philosophic sloven" she was, her "usual dress being a habit of coarse

---

[3] *Analytical Review,* VIII (1790), 254.

[4] John Knowles, *Life and Writings of Henry Fuseli* (3 vols., London, 1831), I, 164.

[5] *Ibid.,* p. 165.      [6] See Paul, *Godwin,* I, 205.

cloth, such as is now worn by milk-women, black worsted stockings, and a beaver hat," and under it "her hair hanging lank about her shoulders."[7] She was thirty years old and had finally, dramatically, made a life-choice: "My die is cast!" she told Everina in 1790; "I could not now resign intellectual pursuits for domestic comforts."[8]

Through all of 1789, then, Mary worked dutifully and diligently as an apprentice writer, reviewing and recommending books that were wholesome and useful, teaching the ways of virtue to young readers, and urging women to be proper mothers and competent members of society. There was no hint that she was resentful in her station, and no one, on the basis of her reviews, would have thought her outside the Bluestocking tradition from Lady Mary Wortley Montagu to Hannah More. But in 1790 Mary exploded out of her women's world and landed squarely in the male arena of political controversy. In her first effort she took on that giant of the English intellectual community, Edmund Burke, in a withering reply to his *Reflections on the French Revolution,* and in the next year, as blazing extension to the *Vindication of the Rights of Men,* she published *The Vindication of the Rights of Woman.* By the following year she was not only famous: in Godwin's words, "perhaps no female writer ever obtained so great a degree of celebrity throughout Europe."[9]

Godwin's description of the French Revolution as a "fundamental shock"[10] was his image of its impact on the English radical community. An electric current it was to Mary, though in truth she was as available and perfect a conductor as, say, her friend Richard Price (whose Old Jewry sermon in 1789 had initially provoked Burke's wrathful denunciation of the revolution and its supporters). The revolution must have been to Mary both a confirmation and a guide: here in France was the example of a people, defined as a nation, taking hold of their destiny, shaping new, appropriate institutions, moving

[7] Knowles, *Fuseli,* I, 165.
[8] Quoted in Wardle, *Wollstonecraft,* p. 109.
[9] Godwin, *Memoirs,* p. 50.     [10] *Ibid.*

through positive, declarative action toward the ideals of sovereignty, of independence and equality of men. The French provided the final proof that one need not accept, acquiesce in, what was, that progress in the society of men need not be left to God's benevolent plan, that men and women could articulate, anticipate, hurry that plan in every awakened corner of the Western world.

From Godwin on, Mary's biographers have not been impressed with *A Vindication of the Rights of Men*. Its faults are glaring: it was an emotional diatribe and a personal attack (on the level of denouncing Burke the placeman, who "in a skulking, unmanly way" had "secured himself a pension of 1,500 pounds per annum on the Irish establishment"),[11] a political polemic written with such speed and anger that its author could not have considered systematic and logical analysis of the text. And yet the public who bought it, who gave it "extraordinary notice," were not so very wrong in the sense that this hitherto unknown Mary Wollstonecraft was someone to be reckoned with. She tore into Burke's arguments for an hereditary aristocratic elite with fury and scorn. "You call yourself a friend of liberty," she wrote; would it "not be more consistent to style yourself the champion of property, the adorer of the golden image which power has set up?"[12] She pointed to Burke's disregard of the hard-working poor with radical indignation: "You have shewn, Sir, by your silence on these subjects, that your respect for rank has swallowed up the common feelings of humanity; you seem to consider the poor as only the live stock of an estate, the feather of hereditary nobility."[13] And in her contempt for what she considered his apostasy from the liberal cause, she denied him his record on the revolution of the American colonies with wild-swinging, scatter-shot invective:

But on what principle Mr. Burke could defend American independence, I cannot conceive; for the whole tenor of his plausible

[11] Mary Wollstonecraft, *A Vindication of the Rights of Men* (London, 1790), p. 20.
[12] *Ibid.*     [13] *Ibid.*, p. 32.

arguments settles slavery on an everlasting foundation. Allowing his servile reverence for antiquity, and prudent attention to self-interest, to have the forces which he insists on, the slave trade ought never to be abolished; and, because our ignorant forefathers, not understanding the native dignity of man, sanctioned a traffic that outrages every suggestion of reason and religion, we are to submit to the inhuman custom, and term an atrocious insult to humanity the love of our country, and a proper submission to the laws by which our property is secured.—Security of property! Behold, in a few words, the definition of English liberty. And to this selfish principle every nobler one is sacrificed. . . . But softly —it is only the property of the rich that is secure; the man who lives by the sweat of his brow has no asylum from oppression; the strong man may enter—when was the castle of the poor sacred?[14]

Maybe this was unfair denunciation, maybe it was, as even Godwin admitted, a "too contemptuous and intemperate" treatment of the "great man" Burke,[15] and maybe it did contain a few "offenses against grammar";[16] still it was a splendid first entry into the arena of political pamphleteering.

And its success must have been the headiest moment of Mary's life. What bliss it must have been to be alive at that revolutionary dawn of 1790, what sustained excitement in reading history in the bare little cell on George Street, or in hotly discussing the latest reports from Paris, or in being an accepted and respected member of a radical vanguard aware of the progress and perfectibility of man and his institutions. Indeed, there must have been months in that year in which Mary had no time to do her hair or buy a new hat; the author of the reply to Burke had world-important things to do.

Specifically she had her own revolutionary area to define, which she did, again at top speed, by producing in six weeks of writing *The Vindication of the Rights of Woman.* (Did Mary, in writing that brilliant book, stop to ask herself in amazement why no woman had said such obvious things before? Or perhaps she knew somehow that it could only have been written in the 1790's?) She addressed herself to the constitu-

[14] *Ibid.,* pp. 23–25.     [15] Godwin, *Memoirs,* p. 51.     [16] *Ibid.,* p. 63.

tional fathers of the new French nation, but her message was directed to the whole of the enlightened West. She demanded, in the first place, that her audience recognize the reality of the historical subjugation of the female half of the human race, and in the second, that room be made for women at the conference table of revolutionary liberalism. Her ideas were simple, her language noninflammatory (contrary to contemporary anti-Jacobins, she did not directly attack the sacrosanct institutions of propertied society—in fact, she thought she was strengthening them—nor did she, in the solemn nonsense of modern psychiatric social adjusters, claim "maleness" for the female). She said that women, too, were God's creatures, and thus reasonable, i.e., perfectible, that women as well as men had the God-given duty of creating themselves as morally responsible individuals, rationally choosing paths of right and virtue. She said further that it had been the historical "tyranny of men" that had denied women their birthright of developing rationality, the male insistence that women as *different* "be kept in ignorance under the specious name of innocence," since they were creatures designed only for "sweet attractive grace, and docile blind obedience."[17] Thus were women restricted to empty-headed gossip, frills and frippery, flirtation and love—and thus in triumph did men point to them as unfit for the serious matters of a progressing civilization. The worst of this was that in consigning half the population—the half responsible for the moral and rational growth of the young—to ignorance and insignificance, male rulers fettered their own progress. Preening themselves as leisured ladies, devoting their days to self-adornment and the gratifications of sensual pleasures—in obedience to male value-makers—women were more and more incapable of the "strength of both body and mind" required by their own "main business," which was the regulation of their families and the education of their children.[18] True social improvement was a patent impossibility until women were aware of and responsible for their duties as wives, mothers, and

[17] Wollstonecraft, *Rights of Woman*, pp. 32-33.    [18] *Ibid.*, p. 137.

citizens. The urgent female need, then, was equality—equality of opportunity, from childhood, to develop themselves physically and mentally, and equality of civil and political rights as adults.[19] In short, Mary had the wit and the courage (and an apparently unique understanding of the meaning of liberal freedom) to expose the hypocrisy of male rhetoric about the natural rights of "mankind," and to insist that women henceforth be included in that generic term. If that logical inclusion would bring a "REVOLUTION in female manners" she was prepared to be considered a revolutionist:

A wild wish has just flown from my heart to my head, and I will not stifle it though it may excite a horse-laugh. —I do earnestly wish to see the distinction of sex confounded in society, unless where love animates the behaviour. . . .

I lament that women are systematically degraded by receiving the trivial attentions, which men think it manly to pay to the sex, when, in fact, they are insultingly supporting their own superiority. It is not condescension to bow to an inferior. So ludicrous, in fact, do these ceremonies appear to me, that I scarcely am able to govern my muscles, when I see a man start with eager, and serious solicitude, to lift a handkerchief, or shut a door, when the *lady* could have done it herself, had she only moved a pace or two.

. . . [Such distinction is], I am firmly persuaded, the foundation of the weakness of character ascribed to woman; is the cause why the understanding is neglected, whilst accomplishments are acquired with sedulous care: and the same cause accounts for their preferring the graceful before the heroic virtues.[20]

Each chapter of Mary's life had ended with a leap, a transcendence, as it were, toward a more ambitious achievement. With the publication of the *Rights of Woman* she got more notoriety than she had dreamed of, personal satisfaction, and the approval and recognition of her (liberal) peers; she had arrived intellectually and, in truth, she had no more intellectual worlds to conquer. Her book was finished at the end of 1791, and for the whole of the following year, in Godwin's words, "she produced nothing, except a few articles in the Analytical

[19] *Ibid.*, pp. 333-335.     [20] *Ibid.*, pp. 120-121.

Review. Her literary meditations were chiefly employed upon the sequel to the Rights of Woman; but she has scarcely left behind a single paper, that can, with any certainty, be assigned to have had this destination."[21] But if she wrote almost nothing in 1792, if she relaxed as a writer, the further truth is that Mary was intensely busy, that she was changing, growing, in other ways.

For one thing, she was adjusting to the status of fame and acclamation. As a perquisite of her literary position she became *Mrs.* Wollstonecraft, and with it came a noticeable shift in life-style. What was happening did not escape a malicious sisterly eye: Eliza wrote to Everina that according to their younger brother Charles, "*Mrs. Wollstonecraft* is grown quite handsome; he adds likewise that being conscious she is on the wrong side of thirty she now endeavours to set off those charms she once despised to the best advantage."[22] Godwin met her for the first time in late 1791 and he must have had some such reaction as this: ". . . those whom curiosity prompted to seek the occasion of beholding her, expected to find a sturdy, muscular, raw-boned virago; and they were not a little surprised, when, instead of all this, they found a woman, lovely in her person, and in the best and most engaging sense, feminine in her manners."[23] Mary *was* a lovely woman, as her portrait by John Opie shows; it was only after her literary triumph that she allowed herself to be aware of it. And she allowed herself to live more graciously and expensively. In September of 1791 she moved to a "large and commodious apartment in Store street, Bedfordsquare" and proceeded to furnish it with a "certain degree of elegance."[24] There was no longer a reason for the "frugality and self-denial" of former years; now that she was an independent woman of sufficient and continuing income, she could afford to live, work, and entertain her friends in pleasant and comfortable surroundings.

Conscious of herself in a new, physical way, relaxing in a

[21] Godwin, *Memoirs*, p. 65.  [22] Paul, *Godwin*, I, 205.
[23] Godwin, *Memoirs*, p. 56.  [24] *Ibid.*, p. 62.

new sense of financial security, indulging herself with a few modest luxuries—here were manifestations of the good life Mary felt she could now enjoy. And—perhaps most apparent to her acquaintances and friends—her ego was developing more expansively than her standard of living. Timidity and self-effacement had never been Mary's first qualities as a professional[25] (or anything else), but with international fame she was positively puffed up with vanity and filled with wonder as she considered her accomplishments. Godwin's account of his meeting with this Mary is too good to abridge:

It was in the month of November in the same year [1791], that the writer of this narrative was first in company with the person to whom it relates. He dined with her at a friend's, together with Mr. Thomas Paine and one or two other persons. The invitation was of his own seeking, his object being to see the author of the Rights of Man, with whom he had never before conversed.

The interview was not fortunate. Mary and myself parted, mutually displeased with each other. I had not read her Rights of Woman. I had barely looked into her Answer to Burke, and been displeased, as literary men are apt to be, with a few offenses against grammar and other minute points of composition. I had therefore little curiosity to see Mrs. Wollstonecraft, and a very great curiosity to see Thomas Paine. Paine, in his general habits, is no great talker; and, though he threw in occasionally some shrewd and striking remarks, the conversation lay principally between me and Mary. I, of consequence, heard her, very frequently when I wished to hear Paine.

We touched on a considerable variety of topics, and particularly on the characters and habits of certain eminent men. Mary, as has already been observed, had acquired in a very blameable degree, the practice of seeing everything on the gloomy side, and bestowing censure with a plentiful hand, where circumstances

---

[25] As Joseph Johnson knew from the beginning of her employment. She told him when he suggested changes in her *Original Stories*, "I cannot *now* concur with you, I mean with respect to the preface, and have not altered it"; and on an assigned review of Samuel Johnson's sermon on the death of his wife, she wrote, "If you do not like the manner in which I review [it], be it known unto you—I *will* not do it any other way." Godwin, *Posthumous Works, Letters to Johnson,* IV, 67–68, 89.

were in any respect doubtful. I, on the contrary, had a strong propensity, to favourable construction, and particularly, where I found unequivocal marks of genius, strongly to incline to the supposition of generous and manly virtues. We ventilated in this way the characters of Voltaire and others, who have obtained from some individuals an ardent admiration, while the greater number have treated them with extreme moral severity. Mary was at last provoked to tell me, that praise, lavished in the way that I lavished it, could do no credit either to the commended or the commender. We discussed some questions on the subject of religion, in which her opinions approached much nearer to the received ones, than mine. As the conversation proceeded, I became dissatisfied with the tone of my own share in it. We touched upon all topics, without reacting forcibly and connectedly upon any.[26]

Mary was not at all abashed by the events of that social evening; apparently her strongest reaction was dislike for that impossible fellow, William Godwin.[27] She was showing off, no doubt, and so taken with herself that she was unaware that her audience was not impressed, that Godwin thought her conversation (and probably her mind) superficial and chaotic. Maybe she deliberately tried to steal the stage from Paine, or maybe she was aggressively annoyed that Godwin didn't know or care to know about her work, which would explain her pose of "seeing everything [that is, Godwin's philosophic radicalism] on the gloomy side." Whatever its impulses, Mary's behavior fit that male-drawn caricature of the "career woman."

Another self-revealing item is a letter written by Mary toward the end of 1792 to an aspiring young author named Mary Hays. The letter began with a few hard remarks about Miss Hays' too effusive attempts to sell her wares to Joseph Johnson—the "cant of both trade and sex," Mary called it—and with the advice that a woman-professional did not have to "behave with the servile obsequiousness of a servant." That out of the way, Mary continued:

I am now going to treat you with still greater frankness. I do not approve of your preface—and I will tell you why. If your work

[26] Godwin, *Memoirs*, pp. 62–64.     [27] *Ibid.*, p. 64.

should deserve attention, it is a blur on the very face of it. Disadvantages of education, etc., ought, in my opinion, never to be pleaded with the public in excuse for defects of any importance, because if the writer has not sufficient strength of mind to overcome the common difficulties which lie in his way, nature seems to command him, with a very audible voice, to leave the task of instructing to those who can. This kind of vain humility has ever disgusted me—and I should say to an author who humbly sued for forbearance, If you have not a tolerably good opinion of your own production, why intrude it on the public? We have plenty of bad books already, that have just gasped for breath and died. The last paragraph I particularly object to—it is so full of vanity. Your male friends will treat you like a woman—and many a man, for instance Dr. Johnson, Lord Littleton, and even Dr. Priestley, have insensibly been led to utter warm eulogiums in private that they would be sorry openly to avow without some cooling explanatory ifs. An author, especially a woman, should be cautious lest she too hastily swallow the crude praises which partial friend and polite acquaintance bestow thoughtlessly when the supplicating eye looks for them. In short, it requires great resolution to try rather to be useful than to please. With this remark in your head, I must beg you to pardon my freedom whilst you consider the purport of what I am going to add—rest on yourself. If your essays have merit, they will stand alone; if not, the *shouldering up* of Dr. this or that will not long keep them from falling to the ground. The vulgar have a pertinent proverb: "Too many cooks spoil the broth"; and let me remind you that when weakness claims indulgence, it seems to justify the despotism of strength. Indeed, the preface, and even the pamphlet, is too full of yourself—inquiries ought to be made before they are answered; and till a work strongly interest the public true modesty should keep the author in the background—for it is only about the character and life of a *good* author that curiosity is active—a blossom is but a blossom.[28]

Mary Hays became and remained Mary's close friend and warm supporter. Perhaps the relationship was fixed on its earliest level, with Mary Wollstonecraft as the successful veteran essayist and Miss Hays as neophyte, pupil, and supplicant

[28] Quoted in *ibid.*, Supplement, p. 175.

(which would remind one of the observation that Mary could only tolerate women "inclined to be subservient to her").[29] Equally possible is Miss Hays' grateful acceptance of Mary's bluntness as honest and quite proper advice: Mary *had* succeeded in a mostly male profession by resting on herself, without obsequiousness and without pleading the disadvantages of her femininity. If there was one thing she knew it was this, the chief focus of her adult reflection: "when weakness claims indulgence, it seems to justify the despotism of strength."

Godwin's point that Mary rebelled against male optimism on enlightened progress, that she ridiculed uncritical praise of "Voltaire and others," may be true. Certain it is, though, that for the moment she had no doubts about herself: in 1791–1792 she was on her own soaring pinnacle of eighteenth-century faith, moving with positive assurance in the clear light of God's rational world. So far had she come from resignation and acceptance of inexplicable fate that all things were possible, for her and perhaps for all the resolute and enlightened, in controlling, improving, changing, one's self and one's society. In the bright glow of personal achievement and liberation, in the euphoria of authorship of the "preliminary sketch of an assumption" of freedom for her sex, Mary felt in such control of her life that there seemed nothing she could not handle. The course of her career was confirmation of what she had once told Joseph Johnson—that nothing she resolved to do remained undone.

[29] *Ibid.*, p. 247. (See above, pp. 14–15, for the full quotation from the journal of Madeleine Schweitzer.)

*Chapter Seven*

# THE INDEPENDENT WOMAN
## PART II

. . . formed for domestic affection [she was] alone, as
it were, in the great mass of her species. . . .
*Memoirs of Mary Wollstonecraft*

What woman essentially lacks today for doing great
things is forgetfulness of herself; but to forget oneself
it is first of all necessary to be firmly assured that now
and for the future one has found oneself.
*The Second Sex*

ONFIDENT, happy, replete—this was Mary's mood in
the aftermath of her polemical success. Or was it?
Four years earlier she had confessed to Joseph
Johnson her sense of the "great defect" in her mind, and of the
"wayward heart" that created its "own misery." "Why I am
made thus I cannot tell," she had said, "and, till I can form
some idea of the whole of my existence, I must be content to
weep and dance like a child—long for a toy, and be tired of it
as soon as I get it."[1] She was still, in 1792, wearing her fool's
cap, though for a time she had felt its weight so little she had
almost forgotten it was there.

Mary had known the painter Henry Fuseli from her first
introduction to Johnson's circle of friends, but it was in 1790
that she became more than casually interested in him. Fuseli
was an artist of considerable reputation, a member of the
Royal Academy, and engaged in the 1790's in completing a
"Milton Gallery," a series of pictures based on Milton's poems;
almost fifty, he had behind him a life of travel and adventure,

[1] Godwin, *Posthumous Works, Letters to Johnson*, IV, 78.

of artistic and literary accomplishment. He was a slight, bushy-browed, white-haired gnome of a man, though Mary was not concerned with his physical appearance. She was entranced by his knowledge and intelligence, by the "poetical imagination" that was so extravagantly evident in his painting, and the "ready wit" and "power and fluency" with words that made him a brilliant guest at the dinner tables of London's radical set. She saw no problem, in the beginning, in the fact that Fuseli was an avowedly happy married man (his wife Sophia was also Mary's friend). Her feeling for him was indeed strong, but, she told herself, it was an intellectual, and thus superior, attraction—all she wanted was to "unite herself with his mind."[2]

Could the second stage in this reasonable infatuation be a surprise to anyone? It was an embarrassment to Mary's heirs: sometime in the nineteenth century a member or members of the Shelley family destroyed her letters to Fuseli;[3] apparently it was felt that this episode was unessential to Mary's history, or in any case that it did not need exposure. Godwin was possibly embarrassed by it too, though in the *Memoirs* he handled it with brief dignity, his honesty more impressive because for reasons of his own he didn't like Fuseli—which is to say that *he* was not attracted to Fuseli's mind. They were such very different men: Godwin with his narrow, rigorous rationalism, Fuseli with a penchant for the fantastic, a passion for Rousseau and what Godwin called the "divinity of genius." Godwin was sure that it had been Fuseli-in-Mary that he had disliked about her the first time he met her at that dinner with Tom Paine, Fuseli the shaping force behind her "contempt" and "cynicism" about the achievements of their century.[4]

But however distasteful he found it, Godwin related the essentials of the story. Mary was "not of a temper," he said, to be close to a man of "merit and genius" without loving him; this was intended as sufficient explanation of the development

[2] Knowles, *Fuseli*, I, 165.
[3] See Wardle, *Wollstonecraft*, p. 350, fn. 8.
[4] Godwin, *Memoirs*, pp. 59–60.

of her admiration into a "personal and ardent affection." Then her feelings for Fuseli became a distraction that turned her thoughts into strange, unprofessional channels: she found herself reflecting that perhaps she was really "formed for domestic affection," that deprived of that domesticity she was "alone, as it were, in the great mass of her species," and spending the "best years of her life" in "comfortless solitude."[5] Wholly inappropriate in relation to Fuseli—given the "Platonic" nature of his regard—such thoughts were intensified, Godwin felt, by the structure of Mary's life, by the "celibacy and restraint" to which "the rules of polished society condemn an unmarried woman."[6] Finally her love, that should have contributed to her intellectual growth and deepened her understanding of art and poetry, that should have been a thing of rational pleasure and joy, became a "perpetual torment," a tangle of emotions so painful that her only solution was to get out of London, "to seek a new climate, and mingle in different scenes."[7]

The one other source of information on this, Mary's first recorded love, is Fuseli's friend and biographer, John Knowles, who claimed that he had or had seen Mary's letters before writing his *Life* of Fuseli. Knowles gave the matter considerable space; in fact, with an ungentlemanly glee, he had a great deal of fun at Mary's expense. In her hot pursuit, he wrote, Mary sent so many letters that Fuseli in indifference and/or disgust left them unopened in his pocket. Knowles found them interesting, however. He reported them full of professions of high-minded passion, with Mary earnestly explaining that though she had "been frequently solicited to marry" she had not done so because she was waiting for a man like Fuseli— someone possessing those "noble qualities, that grandeur of soul, that quickness of comprehension, and lively sympathy" that he so strikingly had.[8] She was abjectly willing, Knowles thought, to change herself to please Fuseli; thus it was because he abhorred the "philosophical sloven" that she became conscious of her appearance and began dressing and living ele-

[5] *Ibid.*, pp. 64–65.   [6] *Ibid.*, pp. 60–61.   [7] *Ibid.*, pp. 64–65.
[8] Knowles, *Fuseli*, I, 163.

gantly (though Fuseli found her no less physically resistible). Throughout the affair, Knowles insisted, Fuseli's behavior was absolutely honorable. He had told Mary from the first that he would only be her friend. Subsequently he tried to reason her out of her infatuation, tried to persuade her to concentrate on her writing (for this was the cause, supposedly, of her nonproductivity after the *Rights of Woman*). But their dialogue proceeded on mutually exclusive planes: Mary talked only of the ethereal quality of her love and her realization that she "was designed to rise superior to her earthly habitation," that she "always thought, with some degree of horror, of falling a sacrifice to a passion which [would] have a mixture of dross in it."[9] Occasionally, perhaps, Fuseli got through to her: in one letter she indignantly told him, "If I thought my passion criminal, I would conquer it, or die in the attempt . . . immodesty, in my eyes, is ugliness; my soul turns with disgust from pleasure tricked out in charms which shun the light of heaven."[10] The climax of the affair, which Knowles related in either amusement or shock (or both), was a scene in which Mary—amazing Mary—called upon Sophia Fuseli and asked permission to live with her and her husband. Precisely, Mary was quoted as saying that because of the "sincere affection" she had for Fuseli "she wished to become an inmate of the family," for she found that she could not live without "the satisfaction of seeing and conversing with him daily." Mrs. Fuseli's reaction was conventional and outraged: she "instantly" ordered Mary out of her house and in essence told her never to come back.[11] The finality of the rejection reached even Mary: on December 8, 1792, she sailed for Paris, leaving behind a letter which begged Fuseli's pardon "for having disturbed the quiet tenour of his life."[12]

Elizabeth Robins Pennell, Mary's staunchly supportive biographer of the 1880's, was furious with Knowles' unflattering tale about her heroine. To "demean" herself with a man, wrote Mrs. Pennell, was "absurdly out of keeping" with Mary's

[9] *Ibid.*, p. 163 fn.    [10] *Ibid.*, pp. 164–167.    [11] *Ibid.*, p. 167.
[12] *Ibid.*, p. 168.

character. Doubtless thinking back to the adolescent who had assumed a "chilling" manner with Fanny Blood when she imagined she was going to "obtrude her affection, or receive love as an alms," Mrs. Pennell was sure that Mary was too "sensitive to slights" to give affection where it was not returned. Knowles, then, had fabricated those humiliating details; perhaps, Mrs. Pennell theorized, the real story was that Fuseli had been at fault, had encouraged Mary to a futile love, and had even gone beyond the proper bounds of a married man, so that Mary had left for Paris "for his sake rather than her own."[13]

Mrs. Pennell's loyalty is a fine thing, and as a testament of stubborn feminism especially appreciated in its 1880's setting. But Mary's memory no longer needs such protectiveness, particularly when it is based on a dismissal not only of Knowles' but of Godwin's quite convincing story of the Fuseli affair. It is preposterous that Godwin might have made up such a story. Besides, and most persuasive, the whole of the evidence, Knowles and Godwin, fits. Here was a Mary in the sophistication of her Age of Reason: no longer the insecure teen-ager who had to control a relationship before exposing her feelings, she was confident that she could relate rationally to rational people, sure even that a rational explanation of her feelings expressed some absolute level of truth that would be as obvious to others as it was to her.

Possibly Mrs. Pennell's problem with the affair was sheer frustration, and a giving up before the inexplicable confusion of Mary's behavior—understandable in the absence of letters, semifictional episodes, or anything that might be more revealing than the Godwin account. She "threw herself" at Fuseli, that modern charge seems clear;[14] but for what longed-for satisfactions, and under what conscious or unconscious impulses? Was the arrogant career woman actually looking for intellectual support, The Word, from an all-prestigious male? (And did she really parrot Fuseli's ideas and assume his atti-

---

[13] Pennell, *Life*, pp. 184–185.
[14] Lundberg and Farnham, *Modern Woman*, p. 160.

tudes, as Godwin thought?—an interesting point, since she would not do that later in her relationship with Godwin.) Beneath her protestations of intellectual admiration was she yearning for a sexual affair with Fuseli, or, in attaching her affections to a married man, was it sex she was anxious to avoid? If she knew she wanted the comforts and companionship of "domesticity," did she see the thorough conventionality of her female equation—love = monogamous relationship + marriagelike nest? And what did she tell herself about her bizarre proposal for a *menage à trois*—that it was a desperate cry from her "wayward heart," or a proudly direct solution from a woman "incapable of disguise"? Mary's behavior, the whole affair, is frustrating, with its provocative clues barely sufficient for speculation.

In the epilogue of her infatuation for Fuseli there is at least the certainty that Mary's solitary voyage to Paris in the early winter of 1792 was a bitter trip. The previous June she had planned a visit to Paris, a wonderful one, to be made with Fuseli (and his wife) and Joseph Johnson. She had written of it to Everina: ". . . For some time past Mr and Mrs Fuseli, Mr Johnson, and myself have talked of a summer excursion to Paris; it is now determined on, and we think of going in about six weeks. I shall be introduced to many people, my book has been translated, and praised in some popular prints, and Mr Fuseli of course is well known; it is then very probable that I shall hear of some situation for Eliza, and I shall be on the watch. . . ."[15] Everina dashed off an excited letter to sister Eliza, who replied in words that were obviously informed of Mary's affairs—and both envious and spiteful:

So the author of "The Rights of Woman" is going to France! I dare say her chief motive is to promote poor Bess's comfort, or thine, my girl, at least I think she will thus reason. Well, in spite of reason, when Mrs W. reaches the Continent she will be but a woman! I cannot help painting her in the height of all her wishes, at the very summit of happiness, for will not ambition fill every chink of her Great Soul (for such I really think hers) that is not

[15] Paul, *Godwin*, I, 206.

occupied by love? After having drawn this sketch, you can hardly suppose me so sanguine as to expect my pretty face will be thought of when matters of State are in agitation, yet I know you think such a miracle not impossible. . . .

And you actually have the vanity to imagine that in the National Assembly, personages like M. and F. will bestow a thought on two females whom nature meant to "suckle fools and chronicle small beer."[16]

More speculative questions: as she sailed alone with her disappointments was Mary self-abusive? Did she berate herself for stupidity and self-delusion, did she feel humiliated or ashamed, would she have been stung by snide sisterly remarks or the gossip of incipient Mrs. Grundys? Or was she merely gloomy, self-pitying, reflecting on her inability to find true love and the predictable mistreatment she received from men? Most likely there was a little of the first and a great deal of the second: Mary obviously felt some contrition about "disturbing" the Fuselis, and somewhere in her self-ruled, self-willed world was an area sensitive to "what people would say." But primarily her old self-righteousness was an excellent device which assured her that she had acted with full purity of motives, that when she realized the hopelessness of her love she had removed herself maturely and quickly (as she had), and that in sum it was Fuseli who had handled it rather badly.[17]

In any case, the one thing quite sure is that she went to Paris to get away from unhappiness, depression, and contemplation of the Fuseli episode, a short visit, as she planned it, with the one aim of distraction. Welcomed as a new member of the international set of friends of the revolution, she had an instant social life with wonderful, committed people—among them Tom Paine, the Americans Mr. and Mrs. Joel Barlow, the Christies (her old friends from the *Analytical Review*), Helen Maria Williams, Jean Caspard Schweitzer and his wife Made-

[16] *Ibid.*, p. 205.
[17] See Knowles, *Fuseli*, I, 169–170, especially a letter written by Mary in 1795, that seems to include Fuseli among the men who had dealt unfairly with her.

leine from Switzerland, the German Count Gustave von Schla-
brendorf, J. G. Forster, who had sailed with Captain Cook,
Thomas Cooper, from Manchester Jacobin circles.[18] By day
she worked to improve her spoken French, wrote the first of a
series of "Letters on the Present Character of the French
Nation" to be published by Joseph Johnson, and began research for a history of the revolution. She was a stunned,
sometimes horrified witness to the stark excitement of the
condemnation of Louis Capet, and of the events prefacing the
English declaration of war against revolutionary France that
made her an enemy alien. Distraction she most certainly had.

But it would be a mistake to assume that the independent
woman of 1790 reappeared from the Fuseli debacle. Whatever
desires had in the beginning drawn her from concentration on
"intellectual pursuits" to the delights of domesticity had been
whetted rather than damped. In the tense, historical atmosphere of revolutionary Paris she was much less concerned
about French than her own affairs, for within four months of
her arrival she was in love with Gilbert Imlay.

[18] Godwin, *Memoirs,* Supplement, pp. 224–226; Wardle, *Wollstonecraft,* p. 184.

# Chapter Eight

# THE WOMAN IN LOVE

Imlay,—dear Imlay,—am I always to be tossed about
thus?—shall I never find an asylum to rest *contented*
in?

Letter to Gilbert Imlay

. . . there are few crimes that entail worse punishment than the generous fault of putting oneself entirely in another's hands.

*The Second Sex*

*M*EASURED against its backdrop of the French Revolution, Mary Wollstonecraft's love affair with Gilbert
Imlay was a petty tale of individual joy and sorrow,
of solitary and isolated infatuation, disappointment, and despair. Yet the historical moment and setting fit: alongside the
world-drama of the classic modern revolution, Mary played
out a fiction-perfect version of the ill-fated love, protagonist in
her own model drama of the *grand amour*. And there is, too, a
fitting parallel of mood: Mary met Imlay in the aftermath of
the trial and execution of Louis Capet. Their affair began
during the Jacobin struggle in the National Convention in
which their faction, the Girondist, was at ominous disadvantage. In the summer of '93, as Mary withdrew to the compara-
tive safety (she was an enemy alien) of a remote cottage
outside Paris, there to live more privately the passion of her
love for Imlay, the Terror in the city was rising to fever pitch
of excitement and radical hope. In September Imlay left
Paris for a shipping business, i.e., "blockade-running,"[1] out of
Havre, his schemes for fortune-making in the capital collapsing

[1] Cameron, ed., *Shelley and His Circle*, I, 127, fn. 25.

with the Girondists. For a few months Mary lived with Imlay at Havre until, in September, 1794, he went to London to new business adventures and less difficult love affairs. Then Mary returned to Paris with their child, her loneliness, her emptiness, appropriate to the end of the Republic of Virtue, and the bourgeois tone of the Thermidorean Reaction.

Mary first met Imlay at the home of Thomas Christie in Paris in April or May of 1793. He was some five years older than she, tall and lanky, an ex-lieutenant in the American revolutionary army, author of a well-reviewed travelogue about the North American West and of a lushly sentimental novel entitled *The Emigrants*.[2] Imlay had come to Paris with letters of introduction to Brissot which recommended him as a key man in the French plan to take the vast Louisiana territory from Spain.[3] Imlay's role in this land-grab possibility, which prominent pro-French Americans—Mary's friend Joel Barlow was one—knew and approved of,[4] was based on his knowledge of the American West; perhaps he was to lead the exploratory expedition across the Mississippi.

At the beginning Mary didn't like Imlay, even avoided meeting him (why?), but dislike "speedily gave place" to a feeling of "greater kindness."[5] By the summer, the mighty events of the revolution swirling over her head, she had committed herself wholly to her love. With Imlay concurring, she moved three miles outside of Paris to the small village of

[2] The travelogue was entitled *A Topographical Description of the Western Territory of North America: Containing a succinct Account of its Soil, Climate, Natural History, Population, Agriculture, Manners and Customs* (London, 1793), and the novel, *The Emigrants, etc., or the History of An Expatriated Family, being a Delineation of English Manners, Drawn from Real Characters* (Dublin, 1794). See the latter, Introduction, Scholars' Facsimiles & Reprints, Robert R. Hare, ed. (Gainesville, Fla., 1964), for the argument that Mary Wollstonecraft was author, part author, or editor of the book.

[3] See Benjamin P. Kurtz and Carrie C. Autrey, eds., *Four New Letters of Mary Wollstonecraft and Helen M. Williams* (Berkeley and Los Angeles, 1937), pp. 32–33.

[4] *Ibid.*; Imlay, *The Emigrants*, p. v.        [5] Godwin, *Memoirs*, p. 68.

Neuilly, taking a tiny cottage so isolated that she saw no one but a local gardener. By day she planned a "great book," that is, a history of the French Revolution, and by night she lived for Imlay. There, far enough from the curiosity of Parisian friends, their love was consummated and there—or more likely at the Barrière, the toll-gate nearest Neuilly, where they met when Imlay was late in leaving the city—their child was conceived.

The secrecy of the affair was maintained until August, when the government issued a decree against English nationals in France, a war measure that put Mary in danger of imprisonment. Imlay, of course, was a citizen of an allied power, and so Mary took his name—there was neither the opportunity nor the impulse for a legal marriage—moved back to Paris and lived openly with him. They had one month together before Imlay left for Havre and his shipping investments. About January, 1794, Mary joined him there, and for the next eight or nine months—little Fanny, the "barrier-girl," "popping" in May—they had a romantic interlude that Mary was sure was the deepest happiness she had ever known. Imlay's business took him late in the summer to London, a temporary separation, as Mary understood it, a necessity of the distasteful "commerce" that was merely the means to the end of acquiring a thousand pounds, the sum that would enable them to buy a farm in America and start life together in the "uncorrupted," "natural" land of liberty.

Even Godwin's ponderous style expressed some part of the inexpressible of Mary's love, and of the transformation that occurred in her in those months of 1793–1794.

Mary now reposed herself upon a person, of whose honour and principles she had the most exalted idea. She nourished an individual affection, which she saw no necessity of subjecting to restraint; and a heart like hers was not formed to nourish affection by halves. . . . Her confidence was entire; her love was unbounded. Now, for the first time in her life, she gave a loose to all the sensibilities of her nature. . . . Her sorrows, the depression of her spirits, were forgotten, and she assumed all the simplicity and vivacity of a youthful mind. She was like a serpent upon a rock, that casts its slough [unhappy metaphor], and appears again with the brilliancy, the sleekness, and the elastic activity of its happiest age. She was playful, full of confidence, kindness and sympathy. Her eyes assumed new lustre, and her cheeks new colour and smoothness. Her voice became chearful; her temper overflowing with universal kindness; and that smile of bewitching tenderness from day to day illuminated her countenance, which all who knew her will so well recollect. . . .[6]

What was it that Mary saw to love so in Gilbert Imlay? No one really knows. One can speculate about Imlay on the fact of his subsequent conduct, but even here one sees him always in the relationship with, and most often through, Mary. Whatever else he may have been, he *was* what Mary made him, the image she created in the first wild passion of her infatuation. Later she would cry out, in anguished momentary recognition of her illusion, that she was "preserving the remembrance of an imaginary being,"[7] but it was not an insight she could hold on to: in her last cold, sad letter to him she would still observe that "in spite of all you do, something like conviction forces me to believe, that you are not what you appear to be."[8] Out of her powerful needs, out of her sense of the deprivation of her past, Mary built a love-figure named Imlay, and made it in all ways a model of excellence.

Thus in Mary's eyes Imlay was a man of estimable character and of intellectual worth. His books were demonstration not only of his solid liberal convictions but of his exquisite "sensibility" as well—particularly *The Emigrants*, which was Mary-like in its thematic presentation of women oppressed by tyrant-males and cruel convention and law. In the privacy of their retreat from Paris, Mary and Imlay must have explored with enormous pleasure their total agreement on all essential matters: the progress of mankind, which was, however unevenly, proceeding everywhere through the spread of education, reason, and liberty; the "sacred truth" of the French

[6] *Ibid.*, pp. 74–75.        [7] Ingpen, ed., *Letters to Imlay*, LXXV.
[8] *Ibid.*, LXXVII.

Revolution, that could not be obscured by the "depravity and weakness" that centuries of tyranny had bred into the French people;[9] the natural equality of women and their natural right to education and life-experience; the corruption that was the traditional institution of property-based marriage. With these qualities of Imlay in mind, Mary would write to her sister from Havre that she was with a "most worthy man, who joins to uncommon tenderness of heart and quickness of feeling, a soundness of understanding and reasonableness of temper rarely to be met with," who, "having been brought up in the interior parts of America," was also "a most natural, unaffected creature."[10]

And Mary admired his strength, that is, his success in varied accomplishments and in dealing with the world—there is nothing in her record that suggests she could have loved someone judged a weakling in social terms. Though before the end of 1793 she had begun to fear and resent the business activities that took him from her, she half-admired his "money-getting face": "I cannot be seriously displeased," she wrote him, "with the exertion which increases my esteem, or rather is what I should have expected from thy character."[11] She had to believe him strong to grant him status as her "protector," to be pleased by the thought that though "she was not a parasite-plant," she "had thrown out some tendrils, to cling to the elm by which she wished to be supported."[12]

This was strange talk from a woman who had all her life used pejorative terms about male strength. That the key to it was sexual is certain. Nowhere to this point in Mary's story has there been a hint of her sexual drives—indeed, even her Freudian analysts admit they "can only guess at the state of her libidinal organization," and then fail to do even that.[13] What was the sexual content of her teen-age religiosity, of the guilt

[9] Mary Wollstonecraft, *An Historical and Moral View of the Origin and Progress of the French Revolution and the Effect it has Produced in Europe* (London, 1794), pp. 492, 512.
[10] Paul, *Godwin*, I, 218.        [11] Ingpen, ed., *Letters to Imlay*, VI.
[12] Godwin, *Memoirs*, pp. 74–75.
[13] Lundberg and Farnham, *Modern Woman*, p. 161.

she said she felt with her mother (but no one else), of her passionate, possessive attachment to Fanny Blood, of her depressions as a young woman, of the Fuseli episode? What were her sexual attitudes when she wrote *Mary*, that tale of disembodied, asexual "sensibility"? What did she know and what did she feel about physical love? Was it only the "dross" of true passion? There is no evidence until Imlay, and then it is overwhelming.

Apparently Imlay was a man of many affairs, perhaps most recently with Helen Maria Williams;[14] he was attracted and attractive to women. It is obvious that he aroused feelings in Mary that she had never felt before, almost as obvious that the intensity of her love surprised them both. "I have thy honest countenance before me," she wrote him when he was in Havre, "—Pop—relaxed by tenderness; a little—little wounded by my whims; and thy eyes glistening with sympathy.—Thy lips then feel softer than soft—and I rest my cheek on thine, forgetting all the world.—I have not left the hue of love out of the picture—the rosy glow; and fancy has spread it over my own cheeks, I believe, for I feel them burning, whilst a delicious tear trembles in my eye. . . ."[15] As early as August, while she was still in Neuilly, there is a note that suggests that her love, perhaps her sexual desire, outraced his: "Cherish me," she wrote, "with that dignified tenderness, which I have only found in you; and your own dear girl will try to keep under a quickness of feeling, that has sometimes given you pain."[16] Almost two years later she put a footnote to the point: "You have sometimes wondered, my dear friend, at the extreme affection of my nature—But such is the temperature of my soul—It is not the vivacity of youth, the hey-day of existence. For years have I endeavoured to calm an impetuous tide—labouring to make my feelings take an orderly course.—It was striving against the stream.—I must love and admire with warmth, or I sink into sadness. Tokens of love which I have

[14] See Ingpen, ed., *Letters to Imlay*, p. xv.  [15] *Ibid.*, VI.
[16] *Ibid.*, II.

received have rapt me in elysium—purifying the heart they enchanted. . . ."[17]

So Mary's sense of Imlay's strength was founded on his accomplishments as a lover, on the intensity of the sexual pleasure she discovered with him. She who had never given herself before gave herself now without restraint; she was indeed enchanted by his love, radiant, ecstatic within it. How in either her conscious or unconscious sense of it could such a love be a casual passing adventure between two independent individuals on the crossroads of revolutionary Paris? It was not simply that Mary, like her mother, like all the females of the "beaten track" she had separated herself from, thought in terms of monogamous love (though of course she did). Her sexual awakening, after so many years of either self-denial and repression or solitary erotic fantasies, was so stunning an occurrence that she could feel its source only in the unique addition to her destiny that was Gilbert Imlay.

In several of her letters to Imlay, Mary referred to herself as "his dear girl" or his "dear *good* girl." "Yes," she wrote in one, "I will be *good*, that I may deserve to be happy, and whilst you love me, I cannot again fall into the miserable state, which rendered life a burthen almost too heavy to be borne."[18] There is so obvious an interpretive possibility here that one can't avoid it, though Simone de Beauvoir has the sensible answer: "The psychoanalysts are wont to assert that woman seeks the father image in her lover; but it is because he is a man, not because he is a father, that he dazzles the girl child, and every man shares in this magical power. Woman does not long to reincarnate one individual in another, but to reconstruct a situation: that which she experienced as a little girl, under adult protection." Mary had not had an idyllic childhood, and she had known little as a girl of "the peace of quasi-passivity." But part of Beauvoir's idea is a neat fit: "Love will give her back her mother as well as her father, it will give her back her childhood. What she wants to recover is a roof over her head,

[17] Wollstonecraft, *Letters from Sweden*, pp. 94–95.
[18] Ingpen, ed., *Letters to Imlay*, II.

walls that prevent her from feeling her abandonment in the
wide world, authority that protects her against her liberty."[19]
Doubtless at some deep level Mary was trying to "reconstruct
a situation" within the felt security of Imlay's love, recreating
a corrected, satisfying childhood scene, complete with warm,
loving, steady, admirable father-figure. There is a suggestion in
some of her letters of something that may relate to unconscious fabrication: she spoke of "glowing with gratitude to
Heaven," or of directing "grateful emotion" to the "Father of
nature, who has made me thus alive to happiness,"[20] as though
she felt a magical quality, a miracle—a basic unreality—of her
love.

Thus Imlay was to Mary in every way a perfect partner: he
loved her and filled all her necessary roles, lover, parent,
friend, intellectual companion; for her it was a relationship that
would be absolute, eternal. There is no evidence that she ever
wanted marriage from him. Though she took his name in Paris
in August of 1793, it was a wartime emergency to keep her out
of prison, not a reflex, at last, of female conditioning. At this
point in her life, in this situation, Mary had a much too exalted
view of the relationship, and too much pride in herself, to
jockey for the trappings of social security. Probably she preferred it without marriage formalities, preferred living with
Imlay in Paris or Havre or waiting for him to make the money
that would send them off to work a farm and raise a family in
America, in what was for both of them a "natural, unaffected"
union. She made no pretense of her legal status when she wrote
to Ruth Barlow in the spring of 1794: "You perceive," she
said, "that I am acquiring the matrimonial phraseology without
having clogged my soul by promising obedience etc etc."[21]
Nor did she really want children: little Fanny (named after
Frances Blood) was an accident; and her happening, bravely as
Mary handled it in her letters, was a difficult problem. In the
fifth month of her pregnancy she wrote in a postscript in a

[19] Beauvoir, *Second Sex*, p. 645.
[20] Ingpen, ed., *Letters to Imlay*, II, VI.
[21] Kurtz and Autrey, eds., *Four New Letters*, p. 41.

note to Imlay: "Finding that I was observed, I told the good women, the two Mrs. ——s simply that I was with child: and let them stare! and —— and ——, nay, all the world, may know it for aught I care! Yet I wish to avoid ——'s coarse jokes."[22] Only a month or so after her birth did the baby become important, a maternal awakening that Mary described in this letter of August, 1794: "I write in a hurry, because the little one, who has been sleeping a long time begins to call for me. Poor thing! when I am sad, I lament that all my affections grow on me, till they become too strong for my peace, though they all afford me snatches of exquisite enjoyment—This for our little girl was at first very reasonable—more the effect of reason, a sense of duty, than feeling—now, she has got into my heart and imagination, and when I walk out without her, her little figure is ever dancing before me."[23]

But if she cared not at all about marriage and very little initially about children, Mary did want "domestic affection" of a demanding kind. It was not that she would abnegate herself, her achievements, her independence (*in toto*), in her love for Imlay. In fact, in the first year of their relationship she completed the first volume of a planned multivolume history of the revolution, a bulky manuscript that Johnson published in 1794 as *An Historical and Moral View of the Origin and Progress of the French Revolution and the Effect it has Produced in Europe*.[24] Mary was no Juliette Drouet who could lose herself in a man-master, nor a Marie d'Agoult (nor a Mary Wollstonecraft Shelley) who could justify herself and her accomplishments in adoration of a male genius. She was still too much the tough-minded woman of her own age, her independence too hard in the winning, to want a self-sacrificial love; this was not the way she sought protection "against her liberty." She wanted an end to the loneliness of her struggle to achieve, she wanted support (though not, pressingly, financial support),[25]

[22] Ingpen, ed., *Letters to Imlay*, X.          [23] *Ibid.*, XXI.
[24] See Kurtz and Autrey, eds., *Four New Letters*, p. 42.
[25] See Cameron, ed., *Shelley and His Circle*, I, 121–129, for evidence that Mary received fifty pounds from Johnson in 1793 in transactions

sympathy, tenderness, understanding, in a relationship that would grant those things necessarily because of its mutuality, a love between equals who would in their individual and united strength protect one another from "abandonment in the wide world." What this meant was an exclusive, possessive love, though Mary would not have called it that; the point of love, as she put it, was "forgetting all the world."

To Fuseli Mary had written that she "was designed to rise superior to her earthly habitation," that she had "always thought, with some degree of horror, of falling a sacrifice to a passion which may have a mixture of dross in it." She intellectualized her affair with Imlay in the same spirit, though, ominously, she had a great deal more to work with. It was her "maxim," as Godwin explained it, that "the imagination should awaken the senses, and not the senses the imagination."[26] That is (and Mary's Romantic soul-mates would later agree), she and Imlay had to build an ideal of their love that would in its celestial grandeur be the stimulus and guide for both sensual passion and the further goal of sustained affection and respect. Sometimes she expressed the thought happily and charmingly, in a letter from Neuilly, for example, in which she anticipated the day "when we are to begin to live together, . . . to try whether we have mind enough to keep our hearts warm."[27] Many times after Imlay's departure she was accusatory and unpleasant in her self-righteous stance that she alone was faithful to their love. She wrote him in 1795:

I shall always consider it as one of the most serious misfortunes of my life, that I did not meet you, before satiety had rendered your senses so fastidious, as almost to close up every tender avenue of sentiment and affection that leads to your sympathetic heart. . . . Ah! my friend, you know not the ineffable delight, the exquisite pleasure, which arises from a unison of affection and desire, when the whole soul and senses are abandoned to a lively imagination, that renders every emotion delicate and rapturous. Yes; these are

through the Paris agent of a British firm; thus she was not dependent on Imlay for support.

[26] Godwin, *Memoirs*, p. 61.        [27] Ingpen, ed., *Letters to Imlay*, II.

emotions, over which satiety has no power, and the recollection of which, even disappointment cannot disenchant; but they do not exist without self-denial. These emotions, more or less strong, appear to me to be the distinctive characteristic of genius, the foundation of taste, and of that exquisite relish for the beauties of nature, of which the common herd of eaters and drinkers and *child-begetters*, certainly have no idea.[28]

No one of Mary's biographers—again, seeing him through her eyes—has dealt kindly with Gilbert Imlay; contemptuously he has been dismissed as a weak, irresponsible tom-cat of a man, "light, heartless, and despicable."[29] Maybe, though, in some part he should be remembered as "poor Imlay." Truly, Mary gave him all of herself; all he was required to give in return was total capitulation to her will. With blind concentration Mary constructed a dream-image, a Mary-Imlay relationship cut whole cloth from her mind and emotions. Indeed, poor Imlay: in Virginia Woolf's gem-phrase, "Tickling minnows he had hooked a dolphin, and the creature rushed him through the waters till he was dizzy and only wanted to escape";[30] and he *had* to escape, for unless he did the creature would turn about and swallow him whole.

What kind of a man was Imlay, and what in the world was he doing with a Mary Wollstonecraft? All we know is the evidence of his actions: child of his age, a liberal, "unspoiled" American, of course he would welcome an affair with an independent, radical, free-thinking woman, the foremost feminist of the day. And certainly he would go along with her notions, share her idealism and "principles" governing their love, even encourage a Rousseauean dream of life in an American rural paradise. But like Joel Barlow, like so many sons of revolutionary fortune, Imlay was an ambitious, money-minded man, to whom the adventure and profit of the export business (shipping even the "soap and alum" Mary referred to with scorn)[31] was the real stuff of life. That is to say, Imlay was a

[28] *Ibid.*, XLIV.        [29] Kurtz and Autrey, eds., *Four New Letters*, p. 33.
[30] Woolf, *Second Common Reader*, p. 145.
[31] Ingpen, ed., *Letters to Imlay*, XXIII.

man to whom love—even Great Love—was but a portion, if a necessary one, of his experience. Apparently he tried to explain these obvious things to an uncomprehending Mary, though he put them in unfortunate words—"living in the present moment," or the "zest for life."[32]

Clearly when Imlay left Havre for London in the fall of 1794, he and Mary were moving on separate tracks, their moment of togetherness lost in the past of Neuilly. Mary, of course, didn't know it; Imlay was her man and her mate and would remain so forever. She wrote soon after he had gone, "I have been playing and laughing with the little girl so long, that I cannot take up my pen to address you without emotion. Pressing her to my bosom, she looked so like you (*entre nous,* your best looks, for I do not admire your commercial face) every nerve seemed to vibrate to the touch, and I began to think that there was something in the assertion of man and wife being one—for you seemed to pervade my whole frame, quickening the beat of my heart. . . ."[33] Did Imlay know it? It would appear so: his business prospered absorbingly in London —the reason that he could not return to France—and for evenings' diversion he took up with a "young actress from a strolling company of players."[34] But if Imlay realized he was done with Mary, he did not tell her so. Perhaps he felt guilt and shame in betraying the idealism he had encouraged. Perhaps he felt responsible for Mary and little Fanny—and Mary's letters of 1795 would work on precisely those feelings, with the partial success that, he said, she "tortured" him.[35] Or perhaps Imlay was neither sensitive nor responsible but simply intimidated, afraid of the formidable woman he had aroused, of the awful force of her dream-love.

One feels a compulsion to hurry through the narration of the final course—it consumed a full year—of Mary's ideal love. From London Imlay wrote asking her to come to England. And she complied reluctantly: ". . . am I only to return to a coun-

[32] *Ibid.,* XXX, XLIV, XXXIV.        [33] *Ibid.,* XXIV.
[34] Godwin, *Memoirs,* p. 81.
[35] Ingpen, ed., *Letters to Imlay,* LXIV.

try, that has not merely lost all charms for me, but for which I
feel a repugnance that almost amounts to horror. . . . Why is it
so necessary that I should return?—brought up here, my girl
would be freer. . . ."[36] Immediately, inevitably, in "pain and
mortification,"[37] she discovered Imlay's affair with the itinerant
young actress. After scenes the emotional punishment of
which one can only guess, Mary threatened or actually
attempted suicide. Imlay was sufficiently worried to devise an
odd scheme: he suggested that Mary take a trip through the
Scandinavian countries, acting there as an authorized emissary
to check his investments and conduct his business. In the
meantime, he told her, he would wind up his unfortunate
liaison and perhaps—the conditional was explicit—meet her in
Switzerland after she had finished the tour. Mary performed
her part of the agreement, came back to England after four
months in Scandinavia, depressed and half-expecting what she
found—Imlay involved as before with business and mistress.
She decided again on suicide, "resolved to plunge herself in the
Thames," but "not being satisfied with any spot nearer to
London, she took a boat, and rowed to Putney."[38] It was
raining when she got there and for an hour longer she walked
about to soak her skirts, then, sodden, flung herself into the
river. Somehow she was saved, pulled senseless from the water,
and taken back to the city. Mrs. Christie offered a bed and care
for a few days, and Imlay, thoroughly frightened, sent a
physician and solace enough that Mary's hopes revived. This
was in October, 1795; for three or four more months she clung
to her illusion that under it all Imlay was the man of Neuilly.
She wouldn't let him go: calling at Christie's with Fanny one
evening, she heard Imlay's voice inside, and brushing aside her
fluttering hostess, marched in, her child by the hand, for a
melodramatic confrontation. At another point she offered
Imlay the suggestion (that only she might have explained) that
she live with him and his mistress "for the sake of the child."

[36] *Ibid.*, XXXVII.      [37] Godwin, *Memoirs*, p. 81.
[38] *Ibid.*, pp. 86–96.

Yet, somehow, something in Mary was working toward health: in the month of March, 1796, she went into the country to the home of an old friend; alone there (and helped by one healingly brutal letter from Imlay) she ended the affair, put Imlay out of her thoughts, and pledged "to make one more effort for life and happiness." "Once after this," Godwin added, "she met Mr. Imlay; probably, not long after her return to town. They met by accident upon the New Road; he alighted from his horse, and walked with her for some time; and the rencounter passed, as she assured me, without producing in her any oppressive emotion."[39]

In the finish there is no problem of "poor Imlay," for whom there need be no sympathy: Mary was the only victim, of her own obsessive self-deception. Her pain and misery in that last year of the affair, not even yet historical abstractions, echo across the decades. One's imagination focusses morbidly on the pages of her letters, that so evoke the hell she made for herself each hour of every day—the racing moments of near-hysterical hope, the agony of the descents into despair, the mind-filling, mind-dulling preoccupation with self. Mary had a terrible talent for self-description in her letters to Imlay, so much aptitude for communicating the anguish he caused her that one half-forgets (though probably Imlay didn't) their unattractive purpose of playing on his guilt. Put into a selected stream, her tormented words are almost more self-exposure than a reader wants:

The train of thoughts which the writing of this epistle awoke, makes me so wretched, that I must take a walk, to rouse and calm my mind. . . . I rather expected to hear from you to-day—I wish you would not fail to write to me for a little time, because I am not quite well—Whether I have any good sleep or not, I wake in the morning in violent fits of trembling—and, in spite of all my efforts, the child—every thing—fatigues me, in which I seek for solace or amusement. . . . I labour in vain to calm my mind—my soul is overwhelmed by sorrow and disappointment. Every thing fatigues me—this is a life that cannot last long. It is you who must

[39] *Ibid.*, pp. 95–96.

determine with respect to futurity—and, when you have, I will act accordingly—I mean we must either resolve to live together, or part for ever, I cannot bear these continual struggles. . . . My heart is so oppressed, I cannot write with precision. . . . I will not distress you by talking of the depression of my spirits, or the struggle I had to keep alive my dying heart.—It is even now too full to allow me to write with composure. . . . I am agitated—my whole frame is convulsed—my lips tremble, as if shook by cold, though fire seems to be circulating in my veins. . . .[40]

And this pathetic phrase is haunting: "Imlay,—dear Imlay,—am I always to be tossed about thus?—shall I never find an asylum to rest *contented* in?"[41]

Even this was not the worst: in those final months of futility Mary deteriorated into the rejected woman—begging, pleading, pressuring, above all, self-pitying. From Copenhagen to the northern Norwegian coast in the fall of 1795, her letters were a trail of degeneration:

I do not understand you. It is necessary for you to write more explicitly—and determine on some mode of conduct.—I cannot endure this suspense—decide—Do you fear to strike another blow? We live together or eternally part!—I shall not write to you again, till I receive an answer to this. I must compose my tortured soul. . . . By what criterion of principle or affection, you term my questions extraordinary and unnecessary, I cannot determine.—You desire me to decide—I had decided. You must have had long ago two letters of mine from _____, to the same purport, to consider.—In these, God knows! there was but too much affection, and the agonies of a distracted mind were but too faithfully pourtrayed! What more then had I to say?—The negative was to come from you.—You had perpetually recurred in your promise of meeting me in the autumn—Was it extraordinary that I should demand a yes, or no? Your letter is written in extreme harshness . . . in it I find not a trace of the tenderness of humanity, much less of friendship.—I only see a desire to heave a load off your shoulders. . . . Do not leave me in suspense. I have not deserved this of you. . . . Do not keep me in suspense.—I expect nothing

[40] Ingpen, ed., *Letters to Imlay*, XLIV, XLV, LIV, LXIV.
[41] *Ibid.*, XLII.

from you, or any human being; my die is cast!—I have fortitude
enough to determine to do my duty; yet I cannot raise my
depressed spirits, or calm my trembling heart.—That being who
moulding it thus, knows that I am unable to tear up by the roots
the propensity to affection which has been the torment of my life
—but life will have an end![42]

Surely these lines should have been read by no one:

I know you are not what you now seem—nor will you always act,
or feel, as you now do, though I may never be comforted by the
change.—Even at Paris, my image will haunt you.—You will see
my pale face—and sometimes the tears of anguish will drop on
your heart. . . . Have but a little patience, and I will remove
myself where it will not be necessary for you to talk—of course,
not to think of me. . . . Yet you will not always forget me.—You
will feel something like remorse, for having lived only for yourself—and sacrificed my peace to inferior gratifications. . . . I
have been most ungenerously treated: but, wishing now only to
hide myself, I shall be silent as the grave in which I long to forget
myself.[43]

The hard question, for Godwin, for Mary's friends, and for
her biographers, is why—why did she hang on furiously and
futilely, waiting, always waiting, when Imlay's indifference
was clear to any objective eye? Why didn't she live the
independence she had once so proudly praised in herself? Why
didn't she mean it when she insisted that she did not "chuse to
be a secondary object," or when she wrote, "let me tell you, I
have my project also—and if you do not soon return, the little
girl and I will take care of ourselves . . . we will not accept
any of your cold kindness—your distant civilities—no; not we.
. . ."[44] The Freudians would reply with a schematic explanation of Mary's hostility and aggressiveness on the one hand,
her masochism on the other. But the relevant answers could be
given by generations of Mary-like women in love, who have
made self-destructive entries into neurotic attachments, who
have gone on to the perilous error of equating love with life,

[42] *Ibid.*, LXV, LXVII, LXVI, LXVIII.
[43] *Ibid.*, LXXIV, LXXII, LXXIII.    [44] *Ibid.*, XXXII, XXX.

with its paralysis of will and action, its certainty that the loss of love means a sickness unto death. Truly, from 1794 to 1796 Mary was desperately ill. The neurotic conflicts of her life soared to feverish intensity in her love for Imlay, and for two years the fever would not subside. The wonder is not that she caught the hopeless and nearly fatal Imlay-disease but that she finally recovered. The wonder is that she could write as the closing line of her last letter to Imlay the convincingly convalescent phrase, "I part with you in peace."[45]

[45] *Ibid.,* LXXVII.

*Chapter Nine*

# THE MOTHER

... she has got into my heart and imagination, and
when I walk out without her, her little figure is ever
dancing before me.

Letter to Gilbert Imlay

Only the woman who is well balanced, healthy, and
aware of her responsibilities is capable of being a
"good" mother.

*The Second Sex*

*M*ARY'S convalescence after the Imlay affair
was brief. She talked and worked herself back
to health, or rather, she built on the basic stubborn
healthiness that had been there during the most wretched
moments of her lonely love. In the final months of 1795 and
the spring of 1796, her energies flowed into three newly absorbing projects: she published one of the best—and best-sell-
ing—of her books, the *Letters from Sweden,* and began again
to work professionally. She discovered enormous pleasure in
caring for her baby, developed, in fact, into a model middle-
class mother, with an impressively "modern" regimen of infant
and child care. And she met and fell in love with William
Godwin—by now the acknowledged philosopher of English
radicalism—and subsequently bore his child. Career, love, and
maternity—each is a separate theme in the story of Mary's last
year and a half. And each offers separate insights into a finally
maturing Mary and into a life finally settling into patterns of
satisfaction and stability.

The maternal Mary is a pleasant topic. To begin, she had in
Fanny's birth a good experience, one that made her a pioneer
propagandist of the simplicity and efficiency of nature's way.

From Havre she wrote Ruth Barlow this description of her labor:

Here I am, my Dear Friend, and so well, that were it not for the inundation of milk, which for the moment incommodes me, I could forget the pain I endured six days ago.—Yet nothing could be more natural or easy than my labour—still it is not smooth work—I dwell on these circumstances not only as I hope it will give you pleasure; but to prove that this struggle of nature is rendered much more cruel by the ignorance and affectation of women. My nurse has been twenty years in this employment, and she tells me, she never knew a woman so well—adding, French-woman like, that I ought to make children for the Republic, since I treat it so slightly—it is true, at first, she was convinced that I should kill myself and my child; but since we are alive and so astonishingly well, she begins to think that the *Bon Dieu* takes care of those who take no care of themselves.[1]

When she finally reached Everina with a letter, she sent the same report: "I managed myself so well that my lying-in scarcely deserved the name. I only rested, through persuasion, in bed one day, and was out a-walking on the eighth."[2]

Mary was thirty-five years old when Fanny was born, and in all her adult years her closest contact with childbirth and infants had been Eliza's tragi-comic experience and Fanny Blood's delivery and almost immediate death. Her own ma-ternity was bound to be fresh and new, in fact, a first of the kind, totally without precedent. Her lightest, most casual remarks informed correspondents of her delight with her production: "let me tell you that I have got a vigorous little girl, and you were so out in your calculation respecting the quantity of brains she was to have, and the skull it would require to contain them, that you made almost all the caps so small I cannot use them; but it is of little consequence for she will soon have hair enough to do without any."[3] In Fanny's fourth month Everina got a report of an indeterminately older

[1] Kurtz and Autrey, eds., *Four New Letters*, p. 43.
[2] Paul, *Godwin*, I, 220.
[3] Kurtz and Autrey, eds., *Four New Letters*, p. 43.

child: "I want you to see my little girl, who is more like a boy. She is ready to fly away with spirits, and has eloquent health in her cheeks and eyes. She does not promise to be a beauty, but appears wonderfully intelligent, and though I am sure she has her father's quick temper and feelings, her good humour runs away with all the credit of my good nursing. . . ."[4]

After Imlay left them at Havre, Mary sent him regular accounts that are mostly revealing of the wonder and pleasure the baby was to her. This, for example, when Fanny was still only four months old: "Besides looking at me, there are three other things, which delight her—to ride in a coach, to look at a scarlet waistcoat, and hear loud music—yesterday, at the *fête*, she enjoyed the two latter; but, to honour J. J. Rousseau, I intend to give her a sash, the first she has ever had round her—and why not? . . ."[5] And at six months, this lovely image: the "little girl, our darling, is become a most intelligent little creature, and gay as a lark, and that in the morning too, which I do not find quite so convenient. I once told you, that the sensations before she was born, and when she is sucking, were pleasant; but they do not deserve to be compared to the emotions I feel, when she stops to smile upon me, or laughs outright on meeting me unexpectedly in the street, or after a short absence."[6]

As the months of Imlay's trips stretched on, Mary's reports turned bittersweet, in regret that the father was missing the marvels of Fanny's first year: "She is all life and motion," Mary told him, "and her eyes are not the eyes of a fool—I will swear. . . . [She is] an affectionate, intelligent creature, with as much vivacity, I should think, as you could wish for."[7] Finally she said outright what was on her mind: "I will own to you that, feeling extreme tenderness for my little girl, I grow sad very often when I am playing with her, that you are not here, to observe with me how her mind unfolds, and her little heart becomes attached!—These appear to me to be true pleas-

[4] Paul, *Godwin*, I, 220.    [5] Ingpen, ed., *Letters to Imlay*, XXIII.
[6] *Ibid.*, XXVII.    [7] *Ibid.*, XXV.

ures—and still you suffer them to escape you, in search of what we may never enjoy."[8]

The line about the "inconvenience" of the baby's waking, "gay as a lark," in the early morning touches on the inevitable problem of substitute child care for a mother who was a professional intellectual. Mary, of course, generally had a servant, but she seems to have had trouble finding a satisfactory nanny for the baby; it was only when Fanny was six months old that she could tell Imlay, "She has now the advantage of having two good nurses, and I am at present able to discharge my duty to her, without being the slave of it."[9] But she continued Fanny's willing half-time slave—not least because she was breast-feeding and did so until the baby was almost a year old. The weaning was more a trauma for the mother than for the child; Mary wrote Imlay, as she sailed to England in April of 1795:

Sweet little creature, I deprived myself of my only pleasure, when I weaned her, about ten days ago.—I am however glad I conquered my repugnance.—It was necessary it should be done soon, and I did not wish to embitter the renewal of your acquaintance with her, by putting it off till we met.—It was a painful exertion to me, and I thought it best to throw this inquietude to rest, into the sack that I would fain throw over my shoulder.—I wished to endure it alone, in short—yet, after sending her to sleep in the next room for three or four nights, you cannot think with what joy I took her back again to sleep in my bosom![10]

Apparently little Fanny took her deprivation in stride: the one follow-up was a cryptic comment that "I have weaned my Fanny, and she is now eating away at the white bread."[11]

Mary's desperation with Imlay did not separate her from the baby, despite the reality of two half-crazed suicide attempts. Fanny was the only thing that kept her sane in the terrible year of 1795; nothing else, she said, "but the sight of her—her playful smiles, which seemed to cling and twine round my

[8] *Ibid.,* XXX.   [9] *Ibid.,* XXVII.   [10] *Ibid.,* XXXVIII.
[11] *Ibid.,* XXXIX.

heart" was of any solace.[12] She had never wanted to bring Fanny back to England: it was in reaction against her own country that she was most fiercely a feminist mama and most prone to "lament" that her "little darling" was a girl.[13] Before she left France Mary had made plans for Fanny in case of her death (alone in Paris, she had fastened on the notion that she had a "galloping consumption"). The baby was to be taken by a "German lady" who had a child of the same age and presumably the same sex, with whom Fanny would be raised much as Mary would have done it herself.[14] Even after she brought the baby to England, she thought of France as the only place to carry out her primary plan, "the independence of my child." "Should a peace take place," she thought, "ready money will go a long way in France—and I will borrow a sum, which my industry *shall* enable me to pay at leisure, to purchase a small estate for my girl.—The assistance I shall find necessary to complete her education, I can get at an easy rate at Paris—I can introduce her to such society as she will like. . . ."[15] In any case, she would not allow Fanny to be oppressed by the "state of her sex"; she would find the means to "protect and provide" for the child.[16]

Little Fanny and Marguerite, the nurse Mary had brought from France, went along on the trip to Scandinavia, though they stayed in lodgings in Gothenburg while Mary travelled about on Imlay's business. The baby was fine (though she was teething and had "suffered during the journey with her teeth")[17] and competently cared for, but as she made her stops in Sweden, Norway, and Denmark, Mary missed her dreadfully, fretted and worried and complained of her own "weak melancholy" about their separation. Finishing her tour and heading back, she wrote: "At Gothenburg I shall embrace my Fannikin; probably she will not know me again—and I shall be hurt if she do not. How childish this is! Still it is a natural feeling. I would not permit myself to indulge the 'thick coming fears' of fondness, whilst I was detained by business.—Yet I

[12] *Ibid.*, LV.     [13] *Ibid.*, XXXI.     [14] *Ibid.*, XXXVI.
[15] *Ibid.*, LXVII.     [16] *Ibid.*, LXXIII.     [17] *Ibid.*, LIV.

never saw a calf bounding in a meadow, that did not remind me of my little froliker."[18]

Back in London in 1795 and absorbed in a new relationship and love with William Godwin, Mary found through and with him even more pleasure in Fanny. When they became lovers, Fanny was two years old and even more "all life and motion," an active, sunny toddler in whose baby vocabulary "Man"—her name for Godwin—was a very big word. Out on her walk Fanny would be "importunate with her 'go this way Mama, me wants to see Man.'" One of her greatest delights was the privilege of dining with Man, something of whose indulgence is revealed in her mother's instructions to him to eat his meat first and let Fanny "come up with the pudding," with the postscript, "Do not give Fanny butter with her pudding."[19]

Probably Godwin obeyed such orders, impressed with Mary's expert motherhood and progressive ideas on child rearing. "The cause," she wrote in the fragmentary beginning of what was to be a treatise on infant care, "which renders children as hard to rear as the most fragile plant, is our deviation from simplicity."[20] Fanny was her experiment plant, and a hardy one—despite a bout with smallpox at four months of age and chicken pox at two and a half years. She caught the first disease at Havre, where, Mary was severely certain, "they" treated the "dreadful disorder very improperly." On the "suggestions" of her own common sense, she handled it herself and saved Fanny "much pain, probably her life, for she was very full, by putting her twice a-day into a warm bath."[21] Perhaps she did the same with the chicken pox, for her medical note on that illness concerned the efforts of the household to prevent Fanny "from tearing herself to pieces."[22] But in good health, and that was most of the time, Fanny was raised with simple routines and a simple diet, much fresh air and exercise

[18] Wollstonecraft, *Letters from Sweden*, p. 143.

[19] Wardle, ed., *Godwin and Mary*, pp. 30, 76.

[20] Godwin, *Posthumous Works, Letters on the Management of Infants*, IV, 56.

[21] Paul, *Godwin*, I, 220 (letter to Everina).

[22] Wardle, ed., *Godwin and Mary*, p. 36.

(without being smothered under layers of clothing) and easy-going discipline. The last point should not be translated as parental passivity. Mary had enormous contempt for "weak, indulgent mothers,"—as she had judged, for example, Danish women to be, who, "having no principle of action to regulate their feelings, become the slaves of infants, enfeebling both body and mind by false tenderness."[23] Perhaps Mary's methods were incidentally indicated in a small matter she related to amuse Godwin of Fanny coming "crowing up stairs to tell me that she did not cry when her face was washed."[24]

In early 1797, when Mary knew she was pregnant with Godwin's child, they—after a period of initial adjustment—were both pleased. This was to be a son, who would be named, naturally, William. In the summer Godwin took a two-week trip with a friend, and his long, affectionate letters never lacked a "salute" to little William, though it was chiefly a concerned plea to his mother to take care of herself as well as him. In one answer Mary reported she was "well and tranquil, excepting the disturbance produced by Master William's joy, who took it into his head to frisk a little at being informed of your remembrance." And she added, out of her serene new happiness, "I begin to love this little creature, and to anticipate his birth as a fresh twist to a knot, which I do not wish to untie. . . ."[25] Mary—and Godwin too, on her word—were sure that this birth, like Fanny's, would be an easy one, which she would handle all the better for her first experience.

There are aspects to Mary's preparations for her second experience in childbirth that are in one sense an aside at this point, but in another, very pertinent. She and Godwin were at the center of circles of people committed to the promise and progress of scientific innovation; both of them had friends prominent in medical science who would have been obvious consultants during her pregnancy and for her delivery. In short, Mary could have had the finest medical advice and care available in England. Her choice was to have the baby at home,

[23] Wollstonecraft, *Letters from Sweden*, p. 202.
[24] Wardle, ed., *Godwin and Mary*, pp. 49–50.    [25] *Ibid.*, p. 82.

attended only by a Mrs. Blenkinsop, matron and midwife of the Westminster Lying-in Hospital. She might have chosen to get aid from a more socially acceptable hospital than the Westminster, the chief purpose of which was "the relief of such poor women as are unable to support the expense of procuring proper assistance at home."[26] She might have opted for the scientific vanguard by having a male surgeon, one of the licentiates in midwifery listed by the Royal College of Physicians, or even Dr. John Clarke, not only "one of the most famous women's physicians of the day"[27] but known to her and Godwin as an author on medical research for Joseph Johnson and an associate of their old friend, Dr. George Fordyce. But she didn't. What seems obvious is that Mary carefully arranged a feminist kind of delivery: she would not have a battery of attendants; she would not be assisted by hospitals catering to the rich and pampered, the "sickly"[28] upper-class women she so disdained; she refused male mid-wives whose usurpation of a profession traditionally female she had perhaps studied and deplored; she would have nothing to do with Dr. Clarke, whose published work included an attack on the ancient "practice of midwifery," the custom of leaving obstetrics in the hands of "ignorant women."[29] When Mrs. Blenkinsop requested help, under the threat of postnatal infection after Mary's long, difficult labor, then the male specialists came. A half dozen distinguished medical men gave Godwin advice; though not in obstetrics, Fordyce took over the case and was in constant attendance; Dr. Clarke was called in toward the end to look at this instance of his specialty of "inflammatory and febrile diseases of lying-in women."[30] But by then it was too late.

Thus Mary and Godwin were wrong twice: little William turned out to be a little Mary, and after her birth Mary died of puerperal fever. It is one of the most frustrating of the unfin-

---

[26] Cameron, ed., *Shelley and His Circle*, I, 186, fn. 6.     [27] *Ibid.*
[28] Wollstonecraft, *Rights of Woman*, p. 55.
[29] Cameron, ed., *Shelley and His Circle*, I, 195, fn. 36.
[30] *Ibid.*, p. 194.

ished chapters of Mary's life that she did not live to raise her girls. Who can tell if she was a "good" mother? Maternity had long been a favorite concern of hers—in abstraction: "one of the grand duties annexed to the female character by nature," she had called it in *The Rights of Woman*. When her own maternal time came, she lived up precisely to her first principles—"nursing her children, and discharging the duties of her station with, perhaps, merely a servant maid to take off her hands the servile part of the household business"[31]—and, most impressive, liked doing it. She discovered, under sometimes appalling emotional burdens, her mother's role to be in actuality as solid a domestic pleasure as she had imagined it in her essays. To be a "good mother," she had written, a woman must have "sense" and "independence of mind,"[32] and if her grasp on those qualities was shaky during Fanny's early months, she none the less handled her baby very well indeed. And Fanny's future looked even brighter: as he did in so many areas, Godwin helped Mary in her mother's role. With his addition to her life she avoided any possibility of venting the bitterness she felt toward Imlay on the child, or, more likely, using her as a compensatory object. But Mary missed the hard ages of motherhood. With adolescent daughters, an unhappy, discontented Mary might have been dominating, overbearing, even hostile (as she was with her sisters, to whom she had once promised "to be a mother"). On the other hand, secure, fulfilled, Mary could have been a splendid model and guide for her girls. In that case, had she lived, and lived in continuing satisfaction with Godwin, cheerful little Fanny would not have grown into the melancholy, introverted young woman who died in suicide. Perhaps even romantic young Mary would not have been driven to elopement at age seventeen with Percy Bysshe Shelley.

[31] Wollstonecraft, *Rights of Woman*, p. 325.    [32] *Ibid.*, p. 346.

*Chapter Ten*

# THE PROFESSIONAL

---

... like the majority of her sex, her studies were desultory and her attainments casual, pursued with little method, under the direction of her taste, or as her feelings took the lead. ...

> Mary Hays, "Mary Wollstonecraft,"
> *Annual Necrology*

Woman's situation inclines her to seek salvation in literature and art. Living marginally to the masculine world, she sees it not in its universal form but from her special point of view. ... Taking an attitude of negation and denial, she is not absorbed in the real: she protests against it, with words.

> *The Second Sex*

---

*A*BSORBED as she was in her last years with maternity and love—especially love, the "want" of her heart —Mary doubtless regarded her profession as a writer as a suboccupation. Still, professional status was an established corner of her identity: even in the end-of-the-affair agony of late 1795, she had attended to the prepublication tasks for her *Letters from Sweden*. By spring, 1796, she emerged from the self-immolation of "Mary Imlay" to resume the bread and butter chores of journalistic assignments, and by the summer of that year she was hard at work on a new novel. For the moment, then, the focus is properly on the professional and her work: first, briefly, the Scandinavian travelogue, and second, and most important, her fictional finale, which is, even in its substantive and stylistic inadequacies, a striking biographical insight.

# I

*Letters from Sweden* was a series of reports to a "friend," that is, Imlay; it was certainly less intimate than her posted letters to him, but just as certainly more personal and subjective than the typical travel journal. In it Mary was self-revealing as always, but rather than relating to Imlay or disintegrating love, the best revelations show the operation of a mind and character still very independent.

One marvelous thing about the book (and the trip itself) is its demonstration that in the midst of her descent into self-pity over Imlay's "brutal" treatment, Mary never for a moment doubted her own toughness and competence. Quite matter-of-factly she started off on a long, sometimes miserably uncomfortable sea voyage with a teething baby and an often hysterical French nurse. Once on Scandinavian ground she set out on a planned itinerary of stops in three countries, on a tour that would have been creditable for an Arthur Young. She travelled about for months, soaking up scenery, observing the people, and dealing with Imlay's business contacts, all the while recording coolly and deliberately as a true daughter of enlightened inquiry.

Thus her travels were, she wrote grandly, the "completion of a liberal education" that had helped her form a "just idea of the nature of man," and their diary, the *Letters from Sweden*, was intended as a description of "the present state of morals and manners" of Norway, Sweden, and Denmark. And that, in a way, it was, if one adds the modifying phrase, "seen through the singularly individualistic views of M. Wollstonecraft."

She wanted, for example, to measure Scandinavian progress toward civilization, to estimate Scandinavian devotion to "the grand causes which combine to carry mankind forward, and diminish the sum of human misery."[1] England and America, she knew, "owe their liberty to commerce, which created a

---

[1] Wollstonecraft, *Letters from Sweden*, Appendix.

new species of power to undermine the feudal system." So far so good—but out of the persuasive force of her own experience in the Paris of the Directory (and especially of her experience with Imlay's "money-getting face"), Mary detested commerce, business, and the businessman. Thus she immediately warned that the English and Americans had to "beware" of the "consequences of commerce," for "the tyranny of wealth is still more galling and debasing than that of rank."[2] Most of the people to whom she had introduction on her tour were businessmen—and most of them she disliked instantly. In Laurvik she met a "group of lawyers," whose "visages," she was certain, were "deformed by vice"; the best to be hoped for was that such "locusts" would disappear "as the people became more enlightened."[3] She had to cross over to Hamburg, and that city she especially deplored: "Mushroom fortunes have started up during the war; the men, indeed, seem of the species of the fungus; and the insolent vulgarity which a sudden influx of wealth usually produces in common minds, is here very conspicuous. . . ."[4]

The people she loved were simple rural folk, like those of Tonsberg in Norway, cottagers whose "natural charm" enchanted her. It was possible, she thought, that England might benefit from imitation of customs of Norwegian coastal farm communities—for one, their proper use of Sunday for play and games, which was "more truly religious than all the stupid stillness which the streets of London ever inspired where the sabbath is so decorously observed. . . . It would even, I think, be a great advantage to the English, if feats of activity, I do not include boxing matches, were encouraged on a Sunday, as it might stop the progress of methodism, and of that fanatical spirit which appears to be gaining ground."[5] (That is an interesting comment: it reminds one that Mary was not only a radical liberal but, at some level, still a member of the established church.) She heard about and wanted to meet even finer

[2] *Ibid.*, p. 170.    [3] *Ibid.*, p. 119.    [4] *Ibid.*, pp. 250–251.
[5] *Ibid.*, p. 113.

people farther north, intelligent, substantial farmers with "none of that cunning to contaminate their simplicity, which displeased me so much in the conduct of the [commercial] people on the sea coast."[6] True, a large part of her pleasure with Norwegian farm folk came from the physical beauty of their land, which periodically moved her to rhapsodic Romantic prose:

Here I have frequently strayed, sovereign of the waste, I seldom met any human creature; and sometimes, reclining on the mossy down, under the shelter of a rock, the prattling of the sea amongst the pebbles has lulled me to sleep. . . . Balmy were the slumbers, and soft the gales, that refreshed me, when I awoke to follow, with an eye vaguely curious, the white sails, as they turned the cliffs, or seemed to take shelter under the pines which covered the little islands that so gracefully rose to render the terrific ocean beautiful. The fishermen were calmly casting their nets; whilst the sea-gulls hovered over the unruffled deep. Every thing seemed to harmonize into tranquillity—even the mournful call of the bittern was in cadence with the tinkling bells on the necks of the cows, that, pacing slowly one after the other, along an inviting path in the vale below, were repairing to the cottages to be milked.[7]

Yet Mary had to admit, to herself and to her readers, that she was not a primitivist, really not even a purist nature-lover: "I am delighted with the romantic views I daily contemplate, animated by the purist air; and I am interested by the simplicity of manners which reigns about me. Still nothing so soon wearies out the feelings as unmarked simplicity. I am, therefore, half convinced, that I could not live very comfortably exiled from the countries where mankind are so much further advanced in knowledge, imperfect as it is, and unsatisfactory to the thinking mind. . . . My thoughts fly from this wilderness to the polished circles of the world."[8] In short, progress was a perplexing thing. Was it better to be in a rural paradise where, however, the natives were the paralyzed puppets of custom and tradition, where when one reasoned "on any subject of

<hr/>

[6] *Ibid.*, pp. 167–168.    [7] *Ibid.*, pp. 93–94.    [8] *Ibid.*, pp. 116–117.

change," one was stopped by protests that the "town would talk"—or in a "civilized" nation like England where "at present the accumulation of national wealth only increases the cares of the poor, and hardens the hearts of the rich"?[9] Mary really had no answer, since she had no real inclination to analyze the problem (though she understood as much, probably, as many of the French Jacobins she had known,[10] or, for that matter, as much as the next generation of Romantic rebels against emerging Victorian Podsnappery). The best she could do was a stubborn restatement of eighteenth-century faith in the transforming power and revolutionary force of freedom in art and science. She put it thus: "I am now more than ever convinced, that it is an intercourse with men of science and artists, which not only diffuses taste, but gives that freedom to the understanding, without which I have seldom met with much benevolence of character."[11] Enlightened intellectuals rather than businessmen were the true heralds of progress, whose work and influence would expose the antiprogressive ugliness, the human corruption and waste, of the scramble for individual status and wealth.

*Letters from Sweden* was Mary's last completed work, in many ways the most mature demonstration of her study of philosophic radicalism, her most sustained commentary on the nature of people and society. Part of it came close to being an objective work which displayed the content of her social radicalism; she was convinced of the shaping role of human environment, of the long-run reality of historical progress (if far short of the Godwin of *Political Justice*, which one can be sure she hadn't read). But even at her most objectively radical, Mary was sobered by her sometime sense that "vice" or even

[9] *Ibid.*, pp. 105, 244.

[10] See Charles Morazé, *The Triumph of the Middle Classes* (Cleveland, Ohio, 1967), pp. 113–117, for a discussion of the deficiencies of the "lawyers" of the French Third Estate, 1789–1794, those revolutionists who succeeded magnificently with "ideas and intellectual concepts" but failed "signally" on the crucial practical problems of economics.

[11] Wollstonecraft, *Letters from Sweden*, pp. 152–153.

"evil" was the "grand mobile of action."[12] She was no philosopher, drawn to abstract constructions of ideal progress; she lived too much in the present, was too involved in introspection, and perhaps was too absorbed and chastened by the mysteries of her own psyche to be inspired by the potential perfectibility of the human animal.

For primarily the book is a personal document, with Mary clearly, unapologetically insisting on the reality and the relevance of her thoughts and emotions. It is the book that most clearly revealed her style, that put her absolutely with the coming century—with representatives of the new generation like the young Southey who admired it extravagantly.[13] Nothing in the spirit of the following passage, for example, could have been written by a William Godwin:

> Chance likewise led me to discover a new pleasure . . . learning to row. . . . I soon became expert, and my train of thinking kept time, as it were, with the oars, or I suffered the boat to be carried along by the current, indulging a pleasing forgetfulness, or fallacious hopes.—How fallacious! yet, without hope, what is to sustain life, but the fear of annihilation—the only thing of which I have ever felt a dread—I cannot bear to think of being no more —of losing myself—though existence is often but a painful consciousness of misery; nay, it appears to me impossible that I should cease to exist, or that this active, restless spirit, equally alive to joy and sorrow, should only be organized dust—ready to fly abroad the moment the spring snaps, or the spark goes out, which kept it together. Surely something resides in this heart that is not perishable—and life is more than a dream.[14]

## II

Mary picked up the pieces of her career in 1796 in an appalling political climate. Egged on by wartime passions and middle-class antirevolutionary hysteria, a calculated force of governmental power had descended on radical reformers, on the

---

[12] Godwin, *Posthumous Works, Letters on the Present Character of the French Nation*, IV, 44–45.

[13] Godwin, *Memoirs*, Supplement, pp. 306–307.

[14] Wollstonecraft, *Letters from Sweden*, p. 96.

whole of the English Jacobin movement. Typically, the people of Mary's literary circles had not been within the organizational stream of corresponding societies and structured Painite agitation, but official reaction against an elastically defined seditious activity was a likely enough possibility that, for example, Joseph Johnson considered very carefully the titles he chose for publication.[15] Perhaps Pitt's ministry would not focus on a mere woman, especially one apparently married to an American citizen, but still it was an ominous and a depressing time to be the author of *The Rights of Woman* and an avowed friend of the French Revolution.

But Mary had to support herself, to "write for independence,"[16] as she put it—she would accept nothing more from Gilbert Imlay, even for Fanny—and gradually she re-established her old habits and contacts. Johnson she had never broken with; she had been in steady communication with him in the publication of the *Letters from Sweden,* and with that done (and Imlay exorcised from her mind), she became assistant editor of the *Analytical Review,* responsible herself for many reviews, and for the assignment of others to various of the journal's contributors. It was a busy job, or so Mary admitted in a review she wrote of a three-volume, 800-page work: she recommended the book to young readers "whose patience is not as often put to the proof, in this way, as that of poor reviewers, condemned to read though dulness, perched on their eyelids, invites to sleep or forgetfulness."[17]

So again, as almost a decade before, Mary had with Joseph Johnson steady earnings and work that was good for her ego and her peace of mind. And with livelihood and therapy assured, she could turn to her own projects; she could begin to think of her own creative product, the ambitious something that might rival *The Rights of Woman* as a contribution to human progress.

Or at any rate, it is possible that Mary contemplated her professional challenge in such a way. Since 1792 she had talked

[15] See Cameron, ed., *Shelley and His Circle,* I, 129.
[16] Paul, *Godwin,* I, 230.    [17] *Analytical Review,* XXIV (1796), 404.

of a sequel to *The Rights of Woman* (or a revision: maybe she was aware of the judgment of even friendly critics, Mary Hays, for one, who wrote that "its style, though frequently rich and glowing, is sometimes inflated, and generally incorrect").[18] Probably she considered it now, but—and this seems a likely speculation—she was frustrated by the realization that she had little more to say in abstract argument and case. Her one volume had put the matter squarely: she had reviewed the male authorities on female inferiority, had more or less logically refuted their prejudices, and had identified the opportunities and freedoms that women required to show what they could do—equal access to education and employment, and full civil rights. (The adequacy of Mary's argument is demonstrated by the bulk of nineteenth-century feminist literature, which goes beyond her only in its response to increasingly complicated economic conditions.) Conceivably she might have done an exploratory survey of the history of feminine activity since, say, the sixteenth century, but that would have taken research concentration alien, undoubtedly, to her temperament, let alone interests. Or she might have done a study of working-class women, women in the trades—again a research job and in an area outside her experience (but a project she might have undertaken had she lived longer). What more, then, could she do that would be other than repetition?

Well—or so Mary may have said to herself—she could write a fictional version of *The Rights of Woman*, a sweeping, artistically designed account of women in the modern world, a thesis novel that in reaching the reading public, even in its present condition of hysterically thoughtless conformity, would be in itself a feminist campaign. It would be constructed, naturally, out of her own knowledge and feeling, but surely Mary was not insecure about that: who was better qualified than she, with her lifetime of articulate, aggressive feminism, with her intense experience and her international observation of the plight of the sex?

[18] Hays, "Mary Wollstonecraft," p. 423.

That such was Mary's thinking as she began *The Wrongs of Woman; or, Maria* is a probability supported by the preface in which she set her purpose, sternly and exactly. The book was to be read, she instructed, not as the mere story of an individual but as the history of women, and as though anticipating a protest that it seemed an unduly sorrowful tale she added, "Was not the world a vast prison, and women born slaves?" Mary was aiming, in short, at a panoramic view of woman's situation. The result was a miniature mosaic of Wollstonecraft fact and fancy, with—interestingly, considering the personal contentment she was finding with Godwin in the last months of her life—but one emotional message. The alternative conclusions she was testing when she stopped work on the book almost exhaust the possibilities of pathos, but not one of them wavers from the theme that woman is born to suffer.

Most of the novel takes place in a room-cell of a "private madhouse" in which the heroine, Maria Venables, wakes from drugged sleep to find herself imprisoned. She knows why: her husband George is trying to force her to give him control of a fortune left to her—legally, to her new-born baby girl—by an uncle. Because of George's villainy and greed, the child has been stolen from Maria (and subsequently dies, probably from neglect) and she is a prisoner, helpless and alone in a (fairly posh) Bedlam grave. But she is not quite alone: an attendant whose name is Jemima—an embittered, hostile woman, but whose manner somehow suggests to Maria that she is "superior to her class"[19]—gradually becomes her friend and accomplice. Jemima allows Maria to meet Henry Darnford, a young man also treacherously held in the asylum, and eventually arranges her escape. The setting is a clumsy contrivance but within it Mary could permit her characters to trace the woeful trail of their experiences.

Jemima tells her story first, and a formidable case study it is of the "wretchedness of situation peculiar to [the] sex"[20] of the lower orders. Jemima was a bastard, her mother an inno-

[19] Godwin, *Posthumous Works*, *Maria*, I, 11.        [20] *Ibid.*, p. 116.

cent servant girl who had died in her birth; starting badly, her life had steadily degenerated. As a child she knew only poverty and filth, neglect and maltreatment. Put out as an apprentice, she was raped by her master, then thrown onto the streets to live by thievery and prostitution. She rose briefly in the latter profession to a job in a "house of ill fame," which was better than the bestiality of the streets; here at least, in an environment in which "vice sought to render itself alluring," for the first time she heard a civilized kind of communication between men and women. Indeed, one of her customers, an elderly "voluptuary" who was also a writer, took her out of the brothel to be his housekeeper-mistress. She learned to read in his library, and picked up critical judgment and taste in talking with him and listening to his discussions with friends. (Mary's description of Jemima's benefactor includes the information that he was an artist of sensitivity who "despised the would-be oracles, the self-elected philosophers, who fright away fancy, while sifting each grain of thought to prove that slowness of comprehension is wisdom."[21] Against whom was that dig directed?).

But this was an interlude in Jemima's destiny. The old man died suddenly, too suddenly to arrange a provision for her, and his relatives saw to her speedy departure. Back on the streets of London, her educational ambitions were a misery-provoking memory, her budding intelligence a mocking, bitter voice. She could talk to no one in her former haunts; she could not find honest work in a trade—she was too clumsy with a needle to get a place in "ready-made linen shops, when so many women, better qualified, were suing for it"[22]—and without a "character," that is, references, she could not hope for a domestic position. A man with her willing industry and intellectual abilities would have been certain of a "decent livelihood," but for her there was only the "most menial bodily labour"—in fact, a place as a washerwoman, on her feet "from one in the morning till eight at night, for eighteen or twenty-pence a

[21] *Ibid.*, p. 106.     [22] *Ibid.*, p. 109.

day." Jemima's despair with her condition forced her to an act that was still shameful for her to relate: she met a tradesman who wanted her to become his mistress and live in his house, though he told her honestly that he had a servant girl there whom he had made pregnant. Jemima imposed the provision that he turn the girl out, whereupon the child committed suicide. Shocked by that into celibacy, Jemima remained at the wash tubs until she hurt her leg and had to go to a hospital. She spent her days in that institution furious with the treatment of the patients. The entrance fee was one guinea, a prohibitive sum indicative of a policy not only exploitive of the poor but self-righteously contemptuous of their illnesses and needs. The point of the place, she said, was "for the accommodation of the medical men and their pupils, who came to make experiments on the poor, for the benefit of the rich."[23] After that experience she was so sure that "the rich and poor" were "natural enemies" that she "stole on principle." She spent six months in prison and went from there to another menial job in a workhouse, "where respectable old people, worn out by immoderate labour, sink into the grave in sorrow, to which they are carried like dogs."[24] Finally, through the workhouse overseer, who had established the institution as a profitable investment, she got the job in the asylum; until she met Maria she had been merely waiting out her dark and dreary days.

Listening in sorrowful sympathy to Jemima's story, Maria was not surprised at its steady beat of misery and hopelessness: she had known, she remembered vividly, servant women in her youth whose poverty and childish ignorance and unprotected situations had brought them equal suffering. Her thoughts flew to her baby, being held she knew not where, lamentably a girl, who might without her mother's help be destined in her own class terms to as wretched a life as Jemima's. If only that child got an education, if only she learned somehow to avoid the special kind of slavery that awaited her. And in her frustration and foreboding Maria began to write her memoirs, allowing

[23] *Ibid.*, pp. 121–122.      [24] *Ibid.*, pp. 122–126.

herself to hope that the record of her six-and-twenty years, her memories and advice, might be preserved to instruct her daughter.

Maria's story of her childhood and youth has a thoroughly familiar ring, especially in its selection of emotional realities. She had hated her father, a domineering retired naval officer, and pitied her weak and submissive mother—when she was not angry with the clear preference the latter had all her life shown for an elder brother (". . . my mother only suckled my eldest brother, which might be the cause of her extraordinary partiality").[25] After the mother's death the father took a mistress, an "artful kind of upper servant," whose aggressive use of her "illegitimate authority" made the house unbearable to Maria. The family's gentry fortunes were sufficient to attract suitors, and to get her "freedom" Maria married one of them, a young man with a promising future in business named George Venables. She knew it was a bad, because wholly expedient, decision, but there was nothing else she could do. She, and her younger sisters too, were talented girls who might have "shone in any profession, had there been any professions for women"; they had had no chance to develop special skills, and as for the trades, they "shrunk at the name of milliner or mantua-maker as degrading to a gentlewoman."[26]

Maria realized immediately that George was stupid, vulgar, and coarse, incapable of generosity of spirit and insensitive to anything that mattered to her. He was besides contemptuous of her ideas and accomplishments, she might have known predictably: "Men who are inferior to their fellow-men, are always most anxious to establish their superiority over women."[27] Predictably, too, he was both sexually demanding and unfaithful. Maria was revolted by George's sexual drives, but not, she wanted her daughter to know, because of conditioned female prudishness. Indeed, she added this for her child's edification: "When novelists or moralists praise as a virtue, a woman's coldness of constitution, and want of pas-

[25] *Ibid.*, p. 157.        [26] *Ibid.*, II, 17.        [27] *Ibid.*, p. 12.

sion; and make her yield to the ardour of her lover out of sheer compassion, or to promote a frigid plan of future comfort, I am disgusted." Such views of female sexuality, she cautioned, were an index of the writer's lack of "fire of the imagination," "active sensibility," and "positive virtue."[28] But despite her warm nature Maria took no lovers, though she might have. She knew herself well enough to admit she "could not coquet with a man without loving him a little," and even that little was a dangerous test of her society's double standard of infidelity. Thinking of the "amiable women" who had been made "outlaws of the world" by the label of adulteress, she was reminded of the core of the problem, which was that the law considered a wife and all she had as her husband's goods, that she was as "much a man's property as his horse, or his ass." "But I must have done," she said, "on this subject, my indignation continually runs away with me."[29] Such was Maria's "freedom" in marriage, the contemplation of which made her explode in fury: "Why was I not born a man, or why was I born at all?"[30]

Maria was too strong a personality to yield to a future of servility. After a particularly outrageous display of the viciousness of George's nature, that shattered for her any responsibility she felt in the relationship, she tore off his ring and announced she was leaving. She was pregnant, but she was strengthened by the support of a wealthy uncle, who not only promised to make her his heir but encouraged her in her daring and independence. The course of her escape was tortuous—false identities, frantic moves, and successive sordid hiding places, with George hunting her "like a felon"—but she thought she had made it. After the birth of her baby and the settling on the child of her uncle's estate, she started out for the real freedom of a life in Italy. At that last moment, almost on shipboard with her baby, she was intercepted, somehow drugged, and carried unconscious to the asylum.

Henry Darnford, like Maria tricked and imprisoned by fortune-seeking relatives, tells enough of his story to make clear

[28] *Ibid.*, pp. 29–30.    [29] *Ibid.*, pp. 37–47.    [30] *Ibid.*, I, 181.

why Maria is attracted to him. He is an educated, cultured man: in the beginning of their friendship Maria is impressed by the quality of the books he lent her (Darnford had been allowed to enter the madhouse in style—with a considerable library) and by the critical intelligence of comments written in their margins. In their hours together—surreptitiously arranged by Jemima—he confessed to Maria his disgust with his previous life. In his youth, sickened by the vulgar superficiality of society and social life, he had rebelled, but he could think of no better way to do it than in pointless self-indulgence, dissolute and self-destructive escapades. He had stumbled into the purchase of a commission in the army, an accidentally positive act that took him to North America and the war with the American colonies. For a time he had gotten so interested in the New World that he had sold his commission and travelled about, even going west into the wilderness. But eventually here, too, was disillusion: the primitive forests bored him and in the cities he found no culture, merely an ostentatious display of wealth. The average American, he thought, combined "a head enthusiastically enterprising, with cold selfishness of heart."[31] So he had left the "land of liberty and vulgar aristocracy, seated on her bags of dollars,"[32] and had returned to England, to the unhappy circumstance of imprisonment in an institution for the insane but at the same time to Maria, to the one true, sweet, and honest association of his life.

Of course Maria and Darnford (ah, Imlay of Neuilly!) consummated their love. Briefly Maria played a little game of assumed "coldness," concealing her love for "fear of outrunning his"; but, assured that she was "beloved," she received him "as her husband" and "he solemnly pledged himself as her protector—and eternal friend."[33] In giving herself, Maria explained to her daughter, she had been "above the little concerns of prudence." And she added a piece of pragmatic advice: "We see what we wish, and make a world of our own —and, though reality may sometimes open a door to misery,

[31] *Ibid.*, pp. 59–60.     [32] *Ibid.*, p. 64.     [33] *Ibid.*, p. 71; II, 127.

yet the moments of happiness procured by the imagination, may, without a paradox, be reckoned among the solid comforts of life."[34]

Finally Jemima managed an escape and all three got to temporary safety in London. As they were planning their departure to Paris, George Venables brought a legal suit against Darnford, charging seduction and adultery. In a way, Maria welcomed legal action, for she was now thinking of divorce and remarriage to Darnford. She had already been distressed by a "volatility" in him—which meant that she knew he was likely to be unfaithful—but she would marry him "according to established rules." Though she was convinced in her view of marriage as "leading to immorality," more compelling was her experience that the "odium of society impedes usefulness" for those who ignored it.[35] Thus she urged Darnford to go alone to Paris—which he did—while she attended to the defense in his court case.

In the reply which Maria wrote against the charges—read in court by her counsel—she reviewed the whole of her history with George Venables, surely unanswerable evidence of criminal maltreatment. She pleaded guilty to the charge of adultery and innocent to that of seduction; there was no act of seduction, she said, for "I voluntarily gave myself." She admitted thereby a transgression against the "policy of artifical society," but she denied the efficacious power of that society: "I wish my country to approve of my conduct," she said, "but, if laws exist, made by the strong to oppress the weak, I appeal to my own sense of justice."[36] By the rules of her own morality, then, by her own sense of right and justice, she claimed a divorce from the monster responsible for the wrongs she had suffered, and for the death of her child; and she demanded freedom to enjoy her fortune and to marry a man who had promised the "protection women in the present state of society want."[37]

The court's response to Maria's statement was a lecture on

[34] *Ibid.*, II, 128.    [35] *Ibid.*, pp. 136–141.    [36] *Ibid.*, pp. 151–152.
[37] *Ibid.*, p. 153.

"the fallacy of letting women plead their feelings, as an excuse for the violation of the marriage-vow." The English nation, the judge warned, would not tolerate "French principles in public or private life." It was "the duty of woman to love and obey the man chosen by her parents and relations," and any breach in that God-given law, however insignificant, however apparently justified, opened "a flood-gate for immorality."[38]

And there the finished part of *The Wrongs of Woman; or, Maria* ends. Mary left several drafts for the conclusion of the novel: Maria granted a decision of separation from bed and board, her uncle's legacy closed to her; Maria saddened by Darnford's butterfly affections; Maria a suicide by laudanum; Maria dying, and hallucinating a meeting with her little girl. But whatever the peroration might have been, its point had been made, ringing and clear: "Why was I not born a man, or why was I born at all?"

One could speculate not on how many but on how few readers have encountered *Maria* since Godwin published it in 1798, though that would be, surely, an irrelevancy. Could there be a more marvelous window into Mary in her thirty-eighth year? Searching in her maturity for transcendent accomplishment, she had decided on a fictional history of women, and what had emerged was a distillation of her experience and emotion, a catalog and synthesis of the most dominating and controlling ideas and feelings of her life. The single-minded narrowness of it is breath-taking. Even its badness—its contrived and artificial structure, its thematic characters—is autobiographically revealing. Mary wanted to write something other than a polemic, wanted to produce in fact a fine novel: in her eulogy in *Annual Necrology*, Mary Hays remarked that "aware of the difficulties which attend this species of composition," Mary had "proceeded slowly, with frequent alterations and careful revisions."[39] But no alteration or revision Mary might have made could solve the basic trouble, which was her inability to make a work of art out of her sense of the hope-

[38] *Ibid.*, pp. 155–157.    [39] Hays, "Mary Wollstonecraft," pp. 456–457.

lessly oppressive trap of the woman's situation. One is reminded of Virginia Woolf's discussion in *A Room of One's Own* of the "state of mind" most "propitious for creative work." The mind of the artist, wrote Mrs. Woolf, "must be incandescent"; that is, all "desire to protest, to preach, to proclaim an injury, to pay off a score, to make the world the witness of some hardship or grievance" is "fired out" and "consumed"; then it is that creativity is "free and unimpeded."[40] Mary's inborn creative equipment was rather less than Shakespeare's—Mrs. Woolf's example—but that is only part of the story of her limitations of talent and imagination. Hers was not a life that encouraged "incandescence" of mind and perception. So unfree and impeded was her consciousness that it couldn't have occurred to her to explore the "wrongs" in a society that had produced types like George Venables or Henry Darnford, or the malevolent judge of Maria's court.

In its initial thrust Mary's feminism was a clear, inevitable accompaniment to the male challenge of the eighteenth-century structure of the ancient regime. Men had rebelled against institutions they had had no hand in erecting, against hierarchies over which they had no control, against a maze of customs, traditions, and laws which fettered their flexing wills. Why should not women do the same? The dark grey picture of female reality that she drew in *The Rights of Woman* was a properly traditional indictment flung out at the oppressors by the challenging group. It was essential to a "preliminary sketch of an assumption" of equality to expose the "specious slavery which chains the very soul of woman, keeping her for ever under the bondage of ignorance"; to scorn a society that made women "proud of their weakness" and well satisfied that they were "protected, guarded from care, and all the rough toils that dignify the mind"; to deplore the waste of discontented women who might have "practiced as physicians, regulated a farm, managed a shop, and stood erect, supported by their own industry, instead of hanging their heads"; and to explain the

[40] Virginia Woolf, *A Room of One's Own* (New York, 1929), pp. 58, 59 (Harbinger edition, 1963).

"herculean task" it was for a woman to "think and act" for herself in the present social state, the "superhuman powers" needed to overcome the "difficulties peculiar to her sex."[41]

Yet the key passages of *The Rights of Woman*—Mary's peak of optimism for change, her high point of liberal expectation—were incompatible with pride and arrogance and revolutionary demand. Who would make the revolution for feminine independence? Mary didn't even bother with women as subjects and actors:

I would then fain convince reasonable men of the importance of some of my remarks; . . . I appeal to their understandings. . . . I entreat them to assist to emancipate their companion, to make her a *help meet* for them. . . . Would men but generously snap our chains, and be content with rational fellowship instead of slavish obedience, they would find us more observant daughters, more affectionate sisters, more faithful wives, more reasonable mothers —in a word, better citizens. We should then love them with true affection because we should learn to respect ourselves. . . .[42]

"Be just then, O ye men of understanding!"[43] It might have been a paraphrase of Daniel Defoe, almost a century before: why not, asked Defoe, allow women education, to make them "*suitable* and *serviceable*" companions? And he added—the tone is heavily jocular—"Bless us! What Care do we take to Breed up a good Horse, and to Break him well! and what a Value do we put upon him when it is done, and all because he should be fit for our use! and why not a Woman!"[44]

Mary's challenge for female emancipation had come in *Maria* to a tangle of futility and anger. Its psychological bases were resentment, envy, and self-doubt, and the corresponding perceptions were blinding. Men, all of them, were always the same, united in their freedom and power and united in their resistance to woman's equality, whether they were deliberate tyrants, overbearing boors and oafs, or charming liars.

[41] Wollstonecraft, *Rights of Woman*, pp. 329, 341.    [42] *Ibid.*, p. 342.
[43] *Ibid.*, p. 451.    [44] Defoe, *Essay upon Projects*, pp. 302–303, 296.

# Chapter Eleven

# THE MARRIED WOMAN

---

. . . I found my evenings solitary, and I wished,
while fulfilling the duty of a mother, to have some
person with similar pursuits, bound to me by affection; and beside, I earnestly desired to resign a name
which seemed to disgrace me.

Letter to Amelia Alderson

The restrictions that education and custom impose on
woman now limit her grasp on the universe; when the
struggle to find one's place in this world is too ar-
duous, there can be no question of getting away from
it. . . .

*The Second Sex*

---

●

*I*N the spring of 1797, in a private ceremony in London's St. Pancras Church, Mary Wollstonecraft
married William Godwin, a union that may literally
have created, as Godwin's friend Thomas Holcroft put it in his
congratulatory response, "the most extraordinary married pair
in existence."[1] The two of them made strange legal partners:
Godwin, in whose major work, *Enquiry Concerning Political
Justice*, marriage was one of the most vicious of man's exploitive institutions, and Mary, who had written in her fiction of
an ideal state in which "there is neither marrying, nor giving in
marriage."[2] But Mary's priorities in 1797 overrode principle,
and Godwin gallantly and lovingly conceded to them. Perhaps
it was just as well. If Mary had to have this formal assurance in
order to build a life with Godwin, it was a good thing. For
with Godwin, in what Virginia Woolf called her most "fruit-

---

[1] Paul, *Godwin*, I, 240.    [2] Wollstonecraft, *Mary*, p. 187.

ful experiment,"[3] Mary had the only totally successful relationship of her life, one that should have given both of them
continuing real satisfaction. Moreover, it was a dynamic relationship, a testing, changing, growing love, that might have
brought to both of them a new steadiness and maturity.

Mary met Godwin again—she had seen him only casually
since that contentious night four years before—in January of
1796. Her old friend and admirer, Mary Hays, brought them
together in an informal supper party in her rooms, perhaps
hoping Mary would find distraction in the man who had
become one of the most provocative intellectuals of the Eng-
lish-French radical community. This time the evening went
well, that is, without hostile exchanges; he emerged with "no
particular effect," Godwin said, except that he found Mary a
much nicer, softer person and felt sympathy for her "anguish"
over Imlay's desertion. Soon after, Mary went into rural retreat to erase Imlay from her mind and to take charge once
more of herself and Fanny. The second task would not be
easier than the first: she hadn't earned much in the two years
of the Imlay affair and was deep in debt, chiefly to Joseph
Johnson. She had to discharge that obligation before she could
work for the life she planned with and for Fanny on the
Continent. Thus in mid-April she was back in London, tempo-
rarily established in Pentonville near Islington in the north of
the city, not far from Somers Town, where Godwin lived.
One day, it was the fourteenth of that month, Godwin remembered, she called at his house; in a few days he returned her
visit, and they became friends. In July Godwin went away for
a month and while he was gone, Mary set aside her idea of
living abroad, "probably without exactly knowing why," re-
claimed the furniture that she had had in storage since her year
in Store Street, and moved to comfortable lodgings in Somers
Town. When Godwin came back they "met with a new
pleasure" and a somehow "decisive preference" for each

[3] Woolf, *Second Common Reader*, p. 148.

other's company. Three weeks later they became lovers, a
natural, easy, mutually obvious transition—"friendship melting
into love."

The above account, as usual, is Godwin's. It is somehow
pathetic that he felt obliged in the second edition of the
*Memoirs* to justify the sequence of those events, as though he
were confronted not only by the scandalized stares of his own
anti-Jacobins but by the latter-day Freudian charge that Mary
"flung herself at men," that she "took the initiative, commit-
ting the unpardonable sexual blunder of depriving the male of
the initiative."[4] Mary's first visit to him, he was aware, was
"deemed a deviation from etiquette; but she had through life
trampled on those rules which are built on the assumption of
the imbecility of her sex; and had trusted to the clearness of
her spirit for the direction of her conduct, and to the integrity
of her views for the vindication of her character. Nor was she
deceived in her trust. . . ." The intimacy that began in the
summer, he added,

was in that mode, which I have always regarded as the purest and
most refined style of love. It grew with equal advances in the
mind of each. It would have been impossible for the most minute
observer to have said who was before, and who was after. One sex
did not take the priority which long-established custom has
awarded it, nor the other overstep that delicacy which is so
severely imposed. I am not conscious that either party can assume
to have been the agent or the patient, the toil-spreader or the
prey, in the affair. When, in the course of things, the disclosure
came, there was nothing, in a manner, for either party to disclose
to the other.[5]

If one had to be made, that was a good enough answer to the
"morality of vulgar minds."[6] So Mary's call upon Godwin had
been unconventional—when in her professional life had she
been conventional about approaching people who interested
her? In the spring of 1796, when (even as she displayed her
wounds publicly as the blameless victim of a treacherous love

[4] Lundberg and Farnham, *Modern Woman*, p. 160.
[5] Godwin, *Memoirs*, pp. 98–99.     [6] *Ibid*., p. 98.

—witness Godwin's sympathy for her "anguish") she was trying to pull herself together as a writer and professional, why should she not be interested in William Godwin, whose published work had made him, during her absence in France, the intellectual leader of the English Left? As for the extension of friendship into physical attraction and love, sexual intimacy was the impulsive and inevitable outcome of feelings building over a period of four months from liking and respect to love. It had happened once before with Imlay—how much more necessary was it to love and be loved in the empty aftermath of that experience? And Mary's needs fit Godwin's, who at forty was searching for a woman (though not, perhaps, a wife) without knowing exactly how to go about it.[7] The quintessential point is that Mary was a perfect woman for Godwin: vivacious, attractive, intelligent, accomplished, indeed, "celebrated"—she was all these things. But most important, she was an aggressive female who disdained the "imbecilities" of her sex, and whose normally warm—she was ready to call it passionate—nature was doubly so in her rebound from Imlay. Godwin the scholar, the philosopher, the "celibate student of forty,"[8] had a flattering circle of lovely ladies from the literary avant-garde, but Mary eclipsed them all. He was enchanted by her nature and needs: her personality (her "great soul") and her history (her "melancholy experience") gave him confidence, brought him alive, as he so plainly said—"I had never loved till now; or, at least, had never nourished a passion to the same growth, or met with an object so consummately worthy."[9]

They did not marry in that summer of 1796. Godwin explained that too, as "ridiculous on the face of it . . . to require the over-flowing of the soul to wait upon a ceremony." Primary for him was his notorious position on the issue, his

[7] Godwin's confusion on the point—whether to marry or not—did not originate with Mary: see Paul, *Godwin*, I, 30-32, for his tentative plans for marriage as a young man; and Ford K. Brown, *The Life of William Godwin* (London, 1926), p. 113, for his thoughts about a proposal to Amelia Alderson.

[8] Brown, *Godwin*, p. 112.    [9] Godwin, *Memoirs*, pp. 100-101.

philosophic rejection of marriage as a corrupt, property-structured institution. Mary, with rather different concerns, had "an extreme aversion" to the "vulgar discussion" that marriage would certainly encourage, given the fact that by casual acquaintances at least she was still being addressed as "Mary Imlay." (As Godwin pointed out, the irony is that after they did marry, Mary was cut by people who pretended shock that she and Imlay had never been legally joined.) They kept their love and their relationship a secret then, and maintained their separate living quarters, social lives, and friends. That separateness—which continued even after their legal marriage—was an unknowing service to the biographical future: from July, 1796, to August 30, 1797, the day of the birth of their daughter and ten days before Mary's death, they communicated in writing, sometimes several times a day. So different from the correspondence to Imlay, the letters were short, elliptical, on Mary's side now and then almost incomprehensible—the written side of a continuing, close, and very private conversation.

The dominant story in the letters is Mary's, and its theme was her need for reassurance, confidence, faith. She had to know that Godwin was no Imlay, that she was not heading for another unbearable disappointment in love. In her first few notes she covered her anxieties with a tone befitting her years and status. She experimented with approach—she was arch, flirtatious, "saucy" (and in this she was also having irreverent fun with his "sapient Philosophership,"[10] with a man known as much for his solemnity as for his intellectual powers). She would twit him about his lady friends, her possible rivals: "I did not wish to see you this evening, because you have been dining, I suppose with Mrs. Perfection, and comparison[s] are odious." Or, "I spent the evening with Mademoiselle Alderson—you, I'm told, were ready to devour her—in your little parlour. Elle est tres jolie—n'est pas?" Or, "As you dine with Mrs. Perfection to day, it would be dangerous, not to remind you of my existence—perhaps—a word then in your ear—

[10] Wardle, ed., *Godwin and Mary*, p. 13.

should you forget, for a moment, a possible *accident* with the most delightful woman in the world, your fealty, take care not to look over your left shoulder—I shall be there—."[11] But Mary was not a devious woman: the affair was not far along before she expressed her momentary hurts and hostilities in straightforward jealous aggression. This, for example, was explicit pressure:

> I want to scold you for not having secured me a better place, because it is a mortification to me to be where I can neither see nor hear. We were thrust into a corner, in the third row, quite as bad as the Gallery—I had trouble enough with my companion without this circumstance; but I am determined to return to my former habits, and go by [my]self and shift for myself—an amusement loses its name when thus conducted.
>
> If you will call on me this morning, and allow me to spend my spite—I will admit you after the play to night.
>
> You and Mrs. I[nchbald] were at your ease enjoying yourselves —while, poor I!—I was a fool not to ask Opie [John Opie, the painter, whose name was linked with Mary's by acquaintances during these months] to go with me. . . .[12]

Love did strange things to William Godwin. Until he met Mary, his personality seemed a consistent development for a man who was "never a boy": he was humorless, imperceptive, "inordinately vain," a "little patronising," even "disagreeable." The one thing about him that baffled his biographer was his attraction, in the decade of his philosophic fame, to desirable and intelligent ladies like Elizabeth Inchbald or Amelia Alderson, Maria Reveley or Mary Hays.[13] But from the beginning he was transformed by acceptance of the roles Mary imposed on him. These, from the first letter he wrote her, were not the words of a humorless, self-centered man:

> . . . your company infinitely delights me . . . every thing that constitutes the bewitching tout ensemble of the celebrated Mary.

[11] *Ibid.*, pp. 11, 12, 23. "Mrs. Perfection" was Elizabeth Inchbald, writer and dramatist, in whom Godwin had been—was still, as far as his friends knew—interested; Amelia Alderson was a charming young writer who later married the painter John Opie.

[12] *Ibid.*, p. 54.    [13] Brown, *Godwin*, p. 112.

. . . Shall I write a love letter? May Lucifer fly away with me, if I do! No, when I make love, it shall be with the eloquent tones of my voice, with dying accents, with speaking glances (through the glass of my spectacles), with all the witching of that irresistible, universal passion. Curse on the mechanical, icy medium of pen & paper. When I make love, it shall be in a storm, as Jupiter made love to Semele, & turned her at once to a cinder. Do not these menaces terrify you?[14]

To be sure, he was sometimes pushed too hard, and sometimes, one guesses, he was hurt by Mary's total oblivion to his needs and insecurities; then he would be irritable. Mary told him in one letter a "pretty little fable" about a "poor Sycamore" that, "her sap mounting" too early in the spring, put out her buds and a "hoar frost" came and shrivelled up her "unfolding leaves."[15] Godwin was neither touched nor amused: "I have no answer to make to your fable," he replied; "I see not . . . its application." In fact (and what did Mary make of this?), "your fable of to day puts an end to all my hopes. I needed soothing, & you threaten me. Oppressed with a diffidence & uncertainty which I hate, you join the oppressors, & annihilate me. . . ."[16] Or, in another letter, early on a November day, Mary wrote:

How do you do this morning—are you alive? It is not *wise* to be cold during a domesticating season, I mean then to dismiss all my frigid airs before I draw near your door, this evening, and should you, in your way from Mr. Carlisle's, *think* of inquiring for the fourth act of Mrs. Inc[hbald]'s comedy—why it would be a pretty mark of attention. —And—entre nous, *little* marks of attention are incumbent on you at present—But—don't mistake me—I do not wish to put you on your mettle. No; I only want to secure a play, of some kind or other, to rouse my torpid spirits, chez vous.[17]

His vanity piqued, Godwin answered stiffly: "Yes, I am alive. Perhaps I am better. I am glad to hear how enchanting & divine

[14] Wardle, ed., *Godwin and Mary*, p. 8    [15] *Ibid.*, pp. 20–21.
[16] *Ibid.*, p. 22.    [17] *Ibid.*, p. 48.

you will appear this evening. —You spoil little attentions by anticipating them."[18]

But if he now and then rebuffed her, Godwin was wholly involved in Mary's problems, and equal, ultimately, to every anxious test she posed. After his reply to her sycamore fable Mary was perhaps stung and ashamed; in any case she told him that she felt "painfully humble." He answered perfectly: "Humble! for heaven's sake, be proud, be arrogant! You are— but I cannot tell what you are. I cannot yet find the circumstance about you that allies you to the frailty of our nature. I will hunt it out."[19] When he left her on the night they first made love, Mary predictably went through a crisis of doubt and terror. "My imagination is for ever betraying me into fresh misery," she wrote on the following day, "and I perceive that I shall be a child to the end of the chapter. . . . Consider what has passed as a fever of your imagination . . . and I—will become again a *Solitary Walker.* . . ."[20] Godwin's immediate return was total reassurance:

. . . I swear to you that I told you nothing but the strict & literal truth, when I described to you the manner in which you set my imagination on fire. . . . I longed inexpressibly to have you in my arms. . . . I see nothing in you but what I respect and adore. . . . Do not hate me. Indeed I do not deserve it. Do not cast me off. Do not become again a *solitary walker.* Be just to me, & then, though you will discover in me much that is foolish and censurable, yet a woman of your understanding will still regard me with some partiality. . . . Suffer me to see you. Let us leave every thing else to its own course. . . . Be happy. Resolve to be happy. You deserve to be so. Every thing that interferes with it, is weakness & wandering; & a woman, like you, can, must, shall, shake it off. . . . Send me word that I may call on you in a day or two. Do you not see, while I exhort you to be a philosopher, how painfully acute are my feelings? I need some soothing, though I cannot ask it from you.[21]

Under such treatment Mary gave herself totally to love, loved being in love, loved being loved. "Now by these presents

[18] *Ibid.,* p. 49.     [19] *Ibid.,* p. 23.     [20] *Ibid.,* p. 15.     [21] *Ibid.,* pp. 16–17.

let me assure you that you are not only in my heart, but my veins, this morning. I turn from you half abashed—yet you haunt me, and some look, word or touch thrills through my whole frame—yes, at the very moment when I am labouring to think of something, if not somebody, else. Get ye gone Intruder! though I am forced to add dear—which is a call back—When the heart and reason accord there is no flying from voluptuous sensations, I find, do what a woman can—Can a philosopher do more?"[22] Their moments of intimacy became so precious that she resented even friendly interlopers who held her to the fiction of the "solitary walker." About the woman whose country asylum had helped her obliterate her Imlay-memories, she wrote: "Mrs. Cotton comes tomorrow. . . . She talks of a *few* days. Mon Dieu! Heaven and Earth!"[23] And early in 1797 sister Everina came for an unfortunate visit (it was to be the sisters' last meeting) that stretched taut Mary's limited patience. "The evenings with her silent," she told Godwin, "I find very wearisome and embarrassing. . . ." On Everina's most welcome day of departure Mary wrote, "I shall go with her to the coach and . . . will be with you about nine, or had you not better *try*, if you can, to while away this evening. Those to come are our own. . . ."[24]

Surely this was the kind of "soothing" Godwin needed; surely that Mary was the "passion" of his austere and egoistic life had mostly to do with the wonderful rewards he got in giving her pleasure—and security. Describing her in the last few months of their love, he noted "the serenity of her countenance, the increasing sweetness of her manners." "She had always possessed," he added, "in an unparalleled degree, the art of communicating happiness, and she was now in the constant and unlimited exercise of it. She seemed to have attained that situation, which her disposition and character imperiously demanded, but which she had never before attained; and her understanding and her heart felt the benefit of it."[25]

Some would say that this was a union of cripples. According

[22] *Ibid.*, p. 33.    [23] *Ibid.*, p. 45.    [24] *Ibid.*, pp. 68–69.
[25] Godwin, *Memoirs*, pp. 107–108.

to the Freudians, "Mary was emotionally forced to strive for power" over men, without which she felt "helpless, then afraid and anxious, then utterly hostile and unhappy."[26] Who would disagree? Especially now, after the Imlay affair, Mary had to know that Godwin was hers, totally possessed and ready to give her absolute and continuing affirmation of devotion. Perhaps she could never have gotten enough. She told him in one note: "I felt hurt, I can scarcely trace why, last night, at your wishing to roll time back. . . . Call me not fastidious; I want to have such a firm *throne* in your heart, that even your imagination shall not be able to hurl me from it, be it ever so active."[27] This possessiveness, this "mastery," continued the Freudians, was "a defense against anxiety that, actually, revolved about her deep doubt of her power as a woman."[28] Of course—in good part, the exhilaration of love for her must have been its revelation of herself as a woman, its evidence that she was worthy on the market of love-exchange. So much was Mary her society's product: Godwin's love confirmed her femininity, and it was a large flaw in her gratification that until April, 1797, the world was not witness to it.[29] Thus their marriage was done quietly, to alleviate the embarrassment of the philosopher who had written of that institution as a "system of fraud."[30] But it was done, and by Mary's wish; she had to have legal recognition, as much of her status as of her pregnancy.[31]

As for the Godwin who permitted this invasion of his actual and emotional privacy, he was proving, by the Freudians, that he was a "psychologically impaired" male. He did more than permit it: after their marriage a Miss Pinkerton displayed what was to Mary an indecent interest in him (Mary was both furious and terrified, and almost incoherent when she referred

[26] Lundberg and Farnham, *Modern Woman*, p. 161.

[27] Wardle, ed., *Godwin and Mary*, p. 35.

[28] Lundberg and Farnham, *Modern Woman*, p. 161.

[29] See Wardle, ed., *Godwin and Mary*, p. 46.

[30] William Godwin, *An Enquiry Concerning Political Justice, and its Influence on General Virtue and Happiness* (2 vols., London, 1796), II, 498.

[31] See Wardle, ed., *Godwin and Mary*, p. 46.

to the "folly and immorality" of the young lady and to Godwin's "mildness" in fostering a "romantic, selfishness, and pam-
per conceit [sic]" that pleased his "vanity"). Godwin told her
he was "fully sensible" of her interpretation of the matter and
agreed that Miss Pinkerton should be informed that their home
was not open to her.[32] In short, Godwin, who had written in
*Political Justice* of the "odious selfishness" and "perpetual
jealousy" that marriage inevitably brought, encouraged, in
fact, actively worked with Mary in her possessiveness.

There is much more on the neurotic nature of this relationship. With loving and steady attention, Godwin validated
Mary's femininity; then he had to deal with her ambivalence to,
even her rejection of, the gift. By January, 1797, Mary was
certain she was pregnant with his child, and her loudest reaction was—in the only apt descriptive word—bitchy. Day after
day she complained—of a "lowness of spirits," of a "fever" of
spirits, of being "unwell," and finally of "the inelegant complaint, which no novelist has yet ventured to mention as one of
the consequences of sentimental distress."[33] It was all quite
clearly Godwin's fault. "It is very tormenting to be thus,
neither sick nor well," especially "as you scarcely imagine me
indisposed"; and "You do not, I think, make sufficient allowance for the peculiarity of my situation."[34] Because Godwin
had "no petticoats to dangle in the snow," Mary lamented the
fate of the whole of her sex: ". . . women are born to suffer
. . . beset with plagues—within—and without . . . certainly
great fools; but nature made them so."[35] It was perfectly clear
what was the matter with her—she exploded at one point,
"What a fine thing it is to be a man!"[36]—but poor Godwin was
baffled: what did he understand of such things? At first, in his
innocence he took it as personal rejection: "You treated me
last night with extreme unkindness," he said, "the more so,
because it was calm, melancholy, equable unkindness. You
wished we had never met; you wished you could cancel all
that had passed between us. Is this, —ask your own heart, —Is

[32] *Ibid.*, pp. 111, 118–119.    [33] *Ibid.*, pp. 53, 58, 60, 64.
[34] *Ibid.*, pp. 64, 60–61.    [35] *Ibid.*, pp. 62, 64.    [36] *Ibid.*, p. 94.

this compatible with the passion of love? Or, is it not the language of frigid, unalterable indifference?" That piece of stupidity made Mary even more bad-tempered: "This does not appear to me just the moment to have written me such a note as I have been perusing," she told him icily; "I am, however, prepared for any thing. I can abide by the consequences of my own conduct, and do not wish to envolve any one in my difficulties."[37] Surely, in allowing himself to be a punching bag for such female moods, Godwin was not a psychologically strong male (nor, to shift the psychoanalytic grounds, an "authentic" man, living his individuality and freedom).

That is one way to look at it. Another is to accept the fact that these were two damaged people, and to go on to appreciation of the fortunate fit of their problems—that is to say, their love. Obviously Mary made up marvelously well for her periodic nagging and irritability, which in any case did not cut deep: "The partner of my life," Godwin wrote, "was too quick in conceiving resentments; but they were dignified and restrained; they left no hateful and humiliating remembrances behind them, and we were as happy as is permitted to human beings."[38] And on matters important to Godwin she made concessions that must have been painful to her. For example, for all her anxieties and possessiveness, for all that she was a "worshipper of domestic life" (and converted the philosopher-Godwin to the profound contentment of domesticity),[39] she yielded to his structural image of their marital life. If traditional marriage was a monopoly that engrossed its principals, the enlightened couple had to find a way to keep it as free an association as imaginatively possible. Thus after April, 1797, they did "not entirely cohabitate"; though they took a house at "No. 29, Polygon, Somers Town," Godwin kept a separate establishment in the nearby Evesham Buildings. And further

[37] *Ibid.*, pp. 59–60.    [38] Paul, *Godwin*, I, 361.
[39] So much so that in the first novel he wrote after her death—*St. Leon: A Tale of the Sixteenth Century* (4 vols., London, 1799)—was a very special tribute to domestic and married life, a modification and partial retraction of his dismissal of that state in *Political Justice*. See *St. Leon*, I, viii–xi.

bowing to his thought, Mary "agreed in condemning the notion, prevalent in many situations in life, that a man and his wife cannot visit in mixed society, but in company with each other." In practice, this agreement meant that they almost never went out together, that they deliberately followed their old, separate social routines and maintained their separate circles of friends. The benefit, as Godwin put it, was that though for the most part they spent their evenings together, they were "in no danger of satiety," and in fact combined "the novelty and lively sensation of a visit, with the more delicious and heartfelt pleasures of domestic life."[40] Such bourgeois bohemianism was a fine thing for Godwin, who added to his preservation of the study and social habits of a lifetime the warmth of totally committed love. And it was for Mary too, for in keeping the bargain she tried valiantly to control her possessiveness. When Godwin took off on a bachelor's holiday in the summer of '97—Mary was six months pregnant—she was generous and understanding of his pleasure with the trip. One of her letters carried these variants on the emotional difficulties of her position: "I am not fatigued by solitude—yet I have not relished my solitary dinner. A husband is a convenient part of the furniture of a house, unless he be a clumsy fixture. I wish you, from my soul, to be rivetted in my heart; but I do not desire to have you always at my elbow—though at this moment I did not care if you were."[41]

The intellectual promise of their relationship is especially intriguing. Godwin, in attitude and action, laid the essential base for harmony and mutual benefit: he assumed, genuinely, openly, naturally, Mary's independence and equality. That is, he lived his anarchism, his radical individualism, in such totality that he cut through her defensive feminism, made it irrelevant. One would guess he was puzzled by her petulance when she complained one day of the mechanics of a domestic household, of difficulties with "the Landlord," and of the "disagreeable business of settling with trades-people," and was baffled by

[40] Godwin, *Memoirs*, pp. 109-110.
[41] Wardle, ed., *Godwin and Mary*, p. 83.

her aggressiveness when she added, ". . . my time appears to me as valuable as that of other persons accustomed to employ themselves . . . [I] feel, to say the truth, as if I was not treated with respect, owing to your desire not to be disturbed."[42] Of course, in Godwin's view, her time was as valuable as his; as far as he was concerned they were both professional writers, both wholly and critically involved in the most important inquiries of their age. Rather than identical, which it certainly was not, their work was complementary. His philosophic studies, his unshakable rationalism, his lucidity of thought and expression, were a nice contrast to Mary's sometimes mystical approaches, her literary interests and headlong polemical style (and her unschooled prose: once he had smoothed her prickly ego on the matter, Godwin undertook to improve her written work, with what Mary wryly referred to—after her vexation had eased—as "grammatical disquisitions").[43] In this passage about the "improvement" Mary was to his intellectual life, Godwin explained his wonder and delight at the interaction of their minds:

We had cultivated our powers . . . in different directions; I chiefly an attempt at logical and metaphysical distinction, she a taste for the picturesque. One of the leading passions of my mind has been an anxious desire not to be deceived. This has led me to view the topics of my reflection on all sides; and to examine and re-examine without end, the questions that interest me.

But it was not merely . . . the difference of propensities, that made the difference in our intellectual habits. I have been stimulated, as long as I can remember, by an ambition for intellectual distinction; but, as long as I can remember, I have been discouraged, when I have endeavoured to cast the sum of my intellectual value, by finding that I did not possess, in the degree of some other men, an intuitive perception of intellectual beauty. I have perhaps a strong and lively sense of the pleasures of the imagination; but I have seldom been right in assigning to them their proportionate value, but by dint of persevering examination, and the change and correction of my first opinions.

[42] *Ibid.,* pp. 74–75.     [43] *Ibid.,* pp. 28, 35.

What I wanted in this respect, Mary possessed, in a degree superior to any other person I ever knew. The strength of her mind lay in intuition. She was often right, by this means only, in matters of mere speculation. Her religion, her philosophy (in both of which the errors were comparatively few, and the strain dignified and generous) were, as I have already said, the pure result of feeling and taste. She adopted one opinion, and rejected another, spontaneously, by a sort of tact, and the force of a cultivated imagination; and yet, though perhaps, in the strict sense of the term, she reasoned little, it is surprising what a degree of soundness is to be found in her determinations. But, if this quality was of use to her in topics that seem the proper province of reasoning, it was much more so in matters directly appealing to the intellectual taste. In a robust and unwavering judgment of this sort, there is a kind of witchcraft; when it decides justly, it produces a responsive vibration in every ingenuous mind. In this sense, my oscillation and scepticism were fixed by her boldness. . . .[44]

In such tribute to Mary's poetical insights, in his esteem for her conversational talents, in his respect and admiration for the "treasures of her mind" and the "virtues of her heart," Godwin was impressively true to his philosophic doctrines. (And the absence in him of unthinking commonplaces of male superiority, even in discussing the intuitive aspects of the female mind, is surely the key to his popularity with talented women.) Indeed, there were in him hard elements of strength: he wanted neither womanly nor wifely echo to his intellectual pursuits—rather, Mary had his undivided support to be as independent as she was capable of being.

It is a strange thing: Godwin was known as a man of intellectual conceit, which worked out to a revealing touchiness and oversensitivity to criticism; yet with Mary he seemed to be operating from a base of solidity and strength. It was not always so with Mary. She respected his mind and valued his judgment, obviously—perhaps too much, for his criticism or even questioning of her work could be crushing. There was

<hr />

[44] Godwin, *Memoirs*, pp. 124–125.

the time he read one of her early manuscripts, and remarked, in her interpretation of his words, that there was a "radical defect" in her "manner of writing," a "worm in the bud," as it were. Mary's reaction was black depression, accompanied, characteristically, by a flood of words: self-examination, excuses, counter-attack. What must she do, then, give up writing? That would be "tantamount to resigning existence," since she had to support herself by her work (given the fact that her "entire confidence" in Mr. Imlay had "plunged" her into "some difficulties") or "go to sleep for ever." That thought brought to mind Joseph Johnson, who had been the "gainer" from all her publications, whatever their dubious merit. And anyhow there was something in her books "more valuable" than in those on which Godwin bestowed "warm elogiums"— more of herself, of her own sensibility and imagination, her "feelings and passions," rather than the "cold workings of the brain on the materials procured by the senses and imagination of other writers." Then she concluded: "I am more out of patience with myself than you can form any idea of, when I tell you that I have scarcely written a line to please myself (and very little with respect to quantity) since you saw my M.S. I have been endeavouring all this morning; and with such dissatisfied sensations I am almost afraid to go into company— But these are idle complaints to which I ought not to give utterance, even to you—I must then have done—."[45]

In short, even as Godwin built her ego and invited—expected—her to be professionally separate but equal, Mary at times was defensively in competition with him. She had a long way to go, to objective appreciation of herself or of him, to an understanding of the honesty with which he approached her work, or to an approach of his work with similar honesty—to an acceptance without rancor, say, of the qualitative difference between *Maria* and *Caleb Williams*. But the best chance Mary had to make that emotional and perceptual journey was with Godwin.

[45] Wardle, ed., *Godwin and Mary*, pp. 28–29.

They were, in sum, a remarkably matched pair. Surely Mary brought to the relationship her most compulsive anxieties, her fears and resentments and insecurities, all of which so sadly contravened any intellectualized ideal of herself. From the near-catastrophic shock the Imlay episode was to her self-esteem and envisioned future, she came flying, a "poor weary bird,"[46] to the refuge Godwin represented, to the "protector" that in the "present state" of society she needed and wanted. Godwin had to deal with the sense of inferiority she had struggled with since her first defeat, in the dim days of her childhood battle for equality with elder brother Edward. It was Godwin's task to compensate for her awareness of the inadequacy of her girl's education and training, for her knowledge that her work had always been marginal to the product of the male achiever, that she had never been equipped to compete in the male world. He took the driving edge of her problems about love, the emotional set that negated her ideal of a union of equals, of two people loving one another in the freedom of mutual tolerance and individual strength. What he had to handle was a love that was possessive, demanding, domineering—and always unfree. And even Godwin was subject to Mary's stereotyped view of men, and to the trait in her that, had she seen it, might have shamed her particularly. Her hardest contempt was directed at the child-female who left the soul-searching of responsible individuality to the male, but her corroding resentment against men fixed her in as childish a bind, in which she judged men harshly for their faults and failures and excused her own. Justified as it was, Mary's resentment—"slave mentality," she would bluntly have called it in other females—was not an emotional basis for adult autonomy and responsibility.

Yet Mary's problems burdened Godwin not at all. She had neither time nor talent for abstract generalization about their relationship, but Godwin must have thought about it a great deal. The patterns of her life fascinated him. Clearly he quer-

[46] *Ibid.*, p. 26.

ied her often about the things he built into the *Memoirs*—the childhood experiences and their resulting emotional syndrome, the processes by which youthful rebellion and its critical insights were transferred to the larger society, and, intellectualized in radical liberalism, became an explosive exposure of social stupidity, prejudice, and injustice. "I shall assiduously cultivate," he had written in *Political Justice*, "the intercourse of that woman whose accomplishments shall strike me in the most powerful manner,"[47] and surely the accomplishments of the author of *The Rights of Woman* (and probably even of the lover of Gilbert Imlay) struck him most powerfully. There is a passage in his novel *St. Leon* (1799) that surely refers to his delight with the unconventional side of his Mary:

> Few women of regular and reputable lives, have that ease of manners, that flow of fancy, and that graceful intrepidity of thinking and expressing themselves, that is sometimes to be found among those who have discharged themselves in a certain degree from the tyranny of custom. There is something irresistibly captivating in that voluptuousness, which, while it assumes a certain air of freedom, uniformly and with preference conforms itself to the dictates of unsophisticated delicacy. A judicious and limited voluptuousness, is necessary to the cultivation of the mind, to the polishing of the manners, to the refining of sentiment, and the development of the understanding; and a woman deficient in this respect, may be of use for the government of our families, but can neither add to the enjoyments, nor fix the partiality, of a man of animation and taste.[48]

Thus Godwin was uniquely prepared to pronounce Mary an "incomparable" woman. If there were inconsistencies in her thought, limitations in her literary work, clumsiness (or chaos) in her style—these were not faults but poignant evidence of the lifelong inequities she had endured. He might have said the same about her possessive and demanding love, had it ever occurred to him to see it in pejorative terms. The philosopher-Godwin rejected utterly the principle—the "grovelling

[47] Godwin, *Political Justice*, II, 502.     [48] Godwin, *St. Leon*, I, 81-82.

principle," the "curse of modern times"[49]—that "human motives are ultimately resolvable into self-love," but it was not as a philosopher that he responded to the pressure Mary put on him. He sensed only her pain and the wretched memories that sometimes betrayed the "virtues of her heart." Most important, her desperate needs—her desperate need of him—awoke feelings of warmth and tenderness that he had never suspected in himself; in this she was his guide and instructor, his mentor in correcting the stringent rationalism of his former understanding of human relations.

Godwin lived—and worked and wrote—for almost four decades after Mary's death, hard, bitter years in which the philosopher-master of "immoralism," atheism, and anarchism was subjected first to savage public abuse and then consigned to oblivion,[50] years of near-poverty and constant money worries, of meanness and pettiness in too many personal relations. "It is not hard to believe," observed one of his biographers, "that, had Mary Wollstonecraft lived, Godwin would have been a wiser philosopher and a better man"[51]—and that seems a safe speculation. Even the English realities of the early 1800's should have been easier to bear with Mary, who brought to him both an intellectual and emotional completeness.

And Mary? What she knew—perhaps the most she knew—before she died was that she was content, content to settle as "femme Godwin," to have a friend and loving companion and husband, as she explained in her duty letter to Amelia Alderson. The fulfillment was absorbing enough: "I must tell you," she wrote Godwin, "that I love you better than I supposed I did, when I promised to love you for ever—and I will add what will gratify your benevolence, if not your heart, that on the whole I may be termed happy. You are a tender, affectionate creature; and I feel it thrilling through my frame giving

[49] William Godwin, *Essays* (London, 1873), pp. 226–227.
[50] Brown, *Godwin*, p. 151.
[51] David Fleisher, *William Godwin, a Study in Liberalism* (London, 1951), p. 35.

and promising pleasure."[52] Chosen, protected, beloved—she would for a time bask in that yearned-for light. And why not? What had she been searching for in her frantic careening around the fringes of the woman's world? Simply, that which Godwin gave her: love for what she was and admiration for what she did. Such was the "pre-historic" reality of her life.

[52] Wardle, ed., *Godwin and Mary*, p. 82.

# AFTERWORD

*P*URELY as a unique event Mary Wollstonecraft's life has continuing appeal, just as she as an individual remains a fascinating, a colorful and contradictory, study. But I called her a model of bourgeois woman and so, primarily, she is to me. Explicitly she claimed the right to define herself—true to the liberal rhetoric of her society— and that claim marked and distinguished her from the majority of her sex. The heart of her rebellion was her rejection of the female design of the Dr. John Gregorys, of the image of proper femininity molded by would-be Pygmalions since, indeed, the mid-sixteenth century.[1] But with that determination to be "free," Mary proceeded to successive revelations of the limits—external and self-imposed—of her freedom. Hers was a life that posed, but did not answer, the question: how does independent-minded bourgeois woman, given, of course, the weight of traditional institutional and psychological prejudice, but given even more her ambivalent relationship to herself and to men, define herself as "free"? The premises of liberal individualism were the initial stimuli for the search for identity, but the fact and the dilemma were that there was no further help to be had from that ideology. In the words of a modern analyst, "Self-made man, in 'granting' a relative emancipation to women, could offer only his self-made image as a model to be equaled."[2] Mary knew well enough that women were not men, and she insisted even that she did not want to "invert" the

---

[1] The story of the male creation of the "new" woman in middle-class society in England in the sixteenth and early seventeenth centuries needs to be told. As a brief indication, however, see Louis B. Wright, *Middle-Class Culture in Elizabethan England* (Ithaca, N.Y., 1935), Ch. XIII.

[2] Erik H. Erikson, *Identity: Youth and Crisis* (New York, 1968), p. 262.

"order of things" between the sexes,[3] but in consequence as a self-making woman she was suspended in an identityless unknown. If she couldn't be and didn't want to be self-made man, what and where were her models for self-creation? What, in short, did she want for herself as a free woman? Such "freedom" was a weary, sometimes an agonizing burden: thus the periods when in relief and abandon Mary retreated to something very close to the male-imposed female role and identity, or when in resentment and frustration she railed against the tyrants who had by their institutions and attitudes made women weak. Perhaps it was the potentially most fruitful aspect of her relationship with Godwin that he, apparently lacking in Pygmalion-like ambitions, might have helped her in her self-definition; or perhaps, at the least, he might have helped her see that, in the "present state of society," freedom and autonomy were male, as well as female, problems.

Mary's life, then, was a middle-class female "situation," though a little more complicated than most. Because she hadn't solved her most pressing problems, hadn't worked anything out for herself, she could hardly be an historical force, could hardly lead or guide others. Her story is an illumination, a mirror, of the others, in its incoherence, confusion, and indecision a magnification of the others.

[3] Wollstonecraft, *Rights of Woman*, pp. 49, 106.

# INDEX

# A Note on the Author

Margaret George is associate professor of history at the University of Illinois, Chicago Circle Campus. She received her Ph.D. from the University of Pittsburgh where she was a Woodrow Wilson Fellow from 1959 to 1961 and an Andrew Mellon Fellow from 1961 to 1963. Her first book, *The Warped Vision, British Foreign Policy, 1933–1939,* was published in 1966.

UNIVERSITY OF ILLINOIS PRESS